EARTH AGE

A New Vision of God, the Human and the Earth

by
Lorna Green

PAULIST PRESS
New York and Mahwah, N.J.

Library of Congress Cataloging-in-Publication Data

Green, Lorna.
    Earth age : a new vision of God, the human, and the earth / by Lorna Green.
        p.   cm.
    Includes bibliographical references.
    ISBN 0-8091-3496-9
    1. Nature—Religious aspects—Christianity.   2. Human ecology—Religious aspects—Christianity.   3. Earth—Religious aspects.   I. Title.
BT695.5.G734   1994
231.7—dc20   94-11594
                                                                          CIP

Published by Paulist Press
997 Macarthur Boulevard
Mahwah, New Jersey 07430

Printed and bound in the
United States of America

Contents

SPIRITUALITY

*For Graham Hitchins
who gave me the strength*

The earth never tires
The earth is rude, silent, incomprehensible at first
Nature is rude, silent, incomprehensible at first
    Be not discouraged, keep on, there are divine
                    things well envelop'd
I swear to you there are divine things more
            beautiful than words can tell.

—Walt Whitman

Preface

Martin Heidegger, earlier in this century, defined a human being as "the animal metaphysicuum," the metaphysical animal.

For some time I have wanted to write a Metaphysics which could be read by everyone, and yet still stand in the venerable tradition of the philosophers. It has taken me twenty-seven years to find out the structure of Being. Here it is, in terms all can understand.

I wish to extend my thanks and appreciation to:

John Joseph Green, my father, now back in the world of Spirit, who gave me the gift of intellect.

Ludwig Edelstein, Emil Fackenheim, Reginald Allen, my teachers of philosophy, who recognized my gifts and nurtured them. I have been a pilgrim among pilgrims, and none of us have served graven images.

Tom Berry, who opened the doors for me from the great tradition of ideas to the living Earth.

Steven Paul Kenny, Steve Dunn, Anne Lonergan, Paul Cusak, Mary Margaret Howard, Linda Nevins and Brian Hamilton of Holy Cross Centre, where much of the work was written; Kathy and Frank Saul, for sharing their plot of the ground; Lou Niznik and Jane Blewett, for inspiration and their dedicated work for the Earth; Quinn Dilkes and Jackie Davies, who share my perspective; Mother Rose Teresa of the Carmelites of Santa Fe, for unfailing prayers and encouragement; John Gainer and Ash Deshpande of the Cape Breton Hospital, who simply wanted me to be myself; Miriam Randall of the Pecos Benedictine Community, New Mexico, who taught me the resurrected Christ; Carmen Gauthier, with whom I have shared all things philosophical; Ken Henwood, my Cornish cousin, who, like me, has married his creativity, and who suggested we were ready for the epic; John and Janet Foster, brother-in-law and sister, who share my love for the Earth, for their dedicated work on her behalf; Winifred Maud Pasco, my mother, who has always believed in me; Don Knight, who is always there for me, my safe harbor.

Jay McDaniel (*Earth, Sky, Mortals, Immortals*), the first male mind to recognize the validity of what I have written here, in terms I would never have applied to myself—"poetic and visionary"—for his unremitting divine enthusiasm and encouragement.

Margaret Lazear, magnificent woman, connoisseur of ideas, who was the first editor to catch the vision, for steadying me and urging me on during the seven year search for the right press for the book.

Paulist Press, which is exactly the right press for a work that develops out of Catholic traditions, but goes beyond them, for their immediate recognition that we belonged together, and in particular, Doug Fisher, editor incomparable, whose changes have almost always improved the manuscript.

Charles Bell of Santa Fe, New Mexico, and Jim Watkins of Margaree Valley, Nova Scotia, for being my companions as I rambled and ranged the vast territory of Being.

The oldest friends of my life: Cynthia Szego, who shares my contemplative path, for teaching me the needs of my Pisces soul; Timothy Gibbon, who always spoke the truth from her own realist perspective; Dorothy Blake—"Midnight Blue, those treasured thoughts of you . . ."—for being the climbing companion of my life.

"We have been friends together." Yes.

Finally, I acknowledge my greatest debt of all, and the deepest love of my life: the living Silences of the Earth, in which I have brooded much of this work. To them: Honor and Praise. May they always be there to heal the wounds in the human soul.

As for me? I nest in the rock. "By Thy sweet scents draw me." The singing heart is the true guide to life.

All peace,

Lorna Green,
Margaree Valley
Nova Scotia
Canada

Foreword by Thomas Berry

We are presently at a unique moment in the story of the planet Earth. This is not simply a human historical moment, but is a transformation moment for the entire complex of life systems on the planet. The human has developed a profound cultural pathology that is leading the human to plunder the planet and exhaust its physical as well as its biological resources without consideration for the limits of capacity for self-renewal. Because this has never previously been experienced by the Earth we do not know its full consequences, or the length of its endurance.

We do know, however, that it cannot continue indefinitely. For the immediate future the human seems to be developing into some strange form of adaptation to its own self-created environment. Already the devastation inflicted on the surrounding world is bringing about an interior devastation within the human itself. With the loss of the outer experience of these various life forms and the natural phenomena that surround us, the inner imaginative experience of humans is being diminished. The sublimity of existence, the range and grandeur of our poetry and music, the entire aesthetic and spiritual experience, all these are becoming more limited—the inner hunger of soul is not satisfied.

Yet a pervasive mood of denial has settled over the western world, especially, for it is precisely in the western world that the difficulties have originated and are being fostered. The universities, those central institutions for providing directions and a sense of values for society, give little indication in their scientific-technological, or their liberal-humanistic, or their political-economic teaching, that they are aware of what is happening. The jurisprudence of our society is thoroughly supportive of the devastation.

This denial goes with a certain autism, an incapacity to recognize or respond to anything outside the human and the supposed human benefit. The surrounding world is a collection of objects to be exploited as fully and as rapidly as possible, with no understanding that nature is an ever-renewing process while mechanistic processes do not in any manner renew themselves. Mechanistic energy is completely entropic. All our massive production has a minimal period of use and is then set aside on the unnumbered junk heaps that exist throughout the planet, or dispersed into the air, or poured into the sea.

This pervasive autism leaves the human with little capacity for experiencing the universe as primarily a communion of subjects rather than as a collection of objects. That communion and reciprocity are the way to life, and exploitation the way to death, is beyond the understanding of a society caught so deeply in its own fixations.

The problem is how to cure the autism: how to establish an education for reciprocity rather than for exploitation; how to bring human communities to function as integral members of an Earth community that will prosper or decline together; how to establish an interspecies jurisprudence as well as an interhuman jurisprudence.

These are the issues that Lorna Green addresses here. She proposes that we reestablish that primordial intimacy between humans and the natural world that we observe in the indigenous people of the world, an intimacy with all the living creatures and all the physical phenomena that constitute the integral reality that we refer to when we speak of the Earth. For every member of the planet and all its natural phenomena exist only in relation to the other members.

Yet it is not only the powers of Earth but the powers of the universe that deserve our reverence, for beyond the Earth the universe itself is the ultimate community of existence. In the phenomenal order only the universe is self-referent. Every other being is universe-referent. Only the universe is a text without context. Every other being exists in the universe context.

Every power in the universe is needed if humans are to have any integral mode of being or if humans are to survive with any degree of fulfillment. The "powers" that govern the world include these vast powers beyond the Earth. These are spiritual as well as physical forces. We need to recover this intimacy with "all our relations."

We might renew those cosmological rituals whereby we integrate our human activities with the great liturgy of the universe. Of special significance is the presentation of new-born infants to the powers of the universe, as the Omaha Indians do, asking their guidance and protection for the infant throughout the course of its life.

There are the voices also. For every being has its own distinctive voice, its own individual voice. The primary law of the universe is that there should exist no two identical beings or two identical voices. Peoples of the twentieth-century industrial world have never, for the most part, heard the voices about them—the voice of the winds, of the mountains and rivers, the voice of the woodlands and the meadows and all the living creatures that inhabit the land and the sea and fly through the air. If they had, they would surely have responded with the awe and reverence that the peoples of the Earth have known from paleolithic times.

In this, indigenous peoples of the world have been wiser than we have been. Although they lived exposed to the elements and were less protected from the heat and the cold, they lived in a larger, a more expansive world, the world of the stars and all the heavenly and earthly phenomena. They communed with spirit powers more vast than we conceive of.

They had a life of the soul that has been diminishing considerably both for ourselves and our children, by the sterile electronic gadgetry of our times, gadgetry that seldom permits us to have any significant presence to the universe about us. With all the beclouded atmosphere of the city around them the children never see the stars, or else they see them only in a misty haze where they can hardly distinguish one from the other. The lighted cities have replaced the starry heavens.

Even the nature films that are shown on our electronic screens are distant, non-threatening, unreal. As Augustine once noted: a picture of food does not nourish. Worst of all, perhaps, is the Disney World substitution of cuddly animals for the challenging presence of creatures in the grandeur of their full personalities in their native habitats.

Until this final decade of the twentieth century there may have been some excuse for what has been happening. Our commercial and industrial society might have been considered some vast experiment into the possibilities of human control over the natural order of the planet. After all, nature herself had placed within the Earth the capacities for all the energy and its uses that we have discovered. If there was petroleum in the Earth, why not use it as energy for our transportation, for fertilizer, for fabrics, for plastic implements, for energy to run our dynamos? Why not make for ourselves a magic world that we would create and control for ourselves, however it affected the other modes of being about us?

Even this would clearly have been insulting to the dignity of the living creatures about us. To dam the rivers on the scale we have done was obviously an insult to the rivers, to tear the mountains apart for their minerals, to clear-cut the forests, to exhaust the soil with excessive demands on its productivity, to ruin the immense fecundity of the oceans of the world; even to think of this creates a revulsion in any sensible person. But to have done all this, and now to observe the consequences in our air and water and soil and living forms with a certain impassive countenance, this obviously is to be seized by a mental distortion beyond anything we have known throughout the centuries.

How address an issue of such magnitude? That is the question that the author of this study has done. She has articulated the nature of the challenge that we confront and has given us a way of responding to the challenge. Her response comes from her own lifetime experience of extensive study, meditation, and living with the land. She has heard the voices. She has known the spirit forces that surround us. She has endured the chill of winter and the heat and irritations of summer. She has shared in the lives that are lived by all the wild creatures. She has activated within herself something of that wild vision that exists in the unconscious depths of the human psyche, the vision experienced by the shamanic personalities that have guided the destinies of peoples since humans first appeared in the margins of the woodlands and the waters of Earth.

Lorna Green is someone to be listened to.

Introduction

Every day our newspapers and magazines carry fresh stories of ecological disasters. We read about the destruction of the rain forest, pollution of the oceans and the atmosphere, the extinction of species. The list is endless.

For the most part we are reacting piecemeal to the crises. Wilderness buffs challenge logging companies, environmentalists tackle big corporations. It is "them" against "us," and divisions run deep.

We need a larger framework in which to comprehend what is happening. We need to understand that it is our collective way of life as a whole that is destroying the Earth. And we need to understand that at the center, the heart of our way of life, with influences rippling out in all directions, is a framework of ideas, a mind-set, a certain way of seeing, evaluating, valuing, which is based on a false view of the universe. We have not been at home in the universe for quite some time.

The Greeks, just 2500 years ago, lived in a comfortable little world with the Earth at the center of the universe, the sun, planets and stars revolving around the Earth in great circles. In such a world, everything human beings did had importance and significance in the scheme of things.

Not so, ourselves. In a scant 2500 years, modern science has totally revised our notions of the universe. The Earth is no longer the center of our universe; even the sun is no longer the center. Instead, our sun is a rather ordinary star, the Earth is a rather ordinary planet, and we are located in the far-off corner of a galaxy in a universe containing billions of galaxies, quite likely, infinite.

That is the modern picture of the universe. No wonder we take refuge from this stark infinity by huddling in our fabricated cities, mesmerizing ourselves with the news of the day and an endless blitz of conversation. Our insignificance in the universe is frightening.

And our modern scientific explanations do not help us at all. Mind has been discarded in favor of the brain. We are material beings, afloat in a vast sea of matter. There is, basically, nothing but the atoms. The poet Rilke said, "We are not at home in our interpreted world." To make matters worse, there is a great tumult on the Earth plane. An old order is passing away, the Piscean age of dualisms is passing away, and a new age is dawning. But we are deeply in and of the universe. In our fabricated cities, we have only forgotten all this.

At this dawning of an age, many things are happening on the human scene. Essentially, the old ideas of the previous age which have formed and structured civilization are hanging on, and many people cling to them, while the new ideas are beginning to flow in. It is like the receding tide meeting the incoming one. All of us are living through the transition, a time of upheaval and dispersion. Just when we all thought we could settle down and enjoy life—"business as usual"—we find ourselves once more uprooted.

Courage, the current of life is ever onward. Scripture has it: "Behold, I renew all things." The human race is passing through the narrow gate of its dark night of the Spirit, which is a time of excruciating purification, but it has an end.

I believe that our picture of the universe is affecting our attitudes toward the Earth, and that our failure to take responsibility for this planet is a function of our cosmology. There is only one imperative binding on all of us now: Earth must survive. And so, I want to retell our story, and draw, for us, a new picture of our place in the universe.

Essentially, Spirit is everywhere. Religious people have always known this, which is why they are so alienated by the scientific account. It is time, now, to bring our various accounts together, to make sense of ourselves.

We would not be here if the universe did not want us here. We belong. It is time to fully spell out the underpinnings of these intuitions. We are, at present, living out a false metaphysics which is shaping our attitudes to ourselves, each other, and the planet, and the crisis in Earth is telling us this.

If we are to save this planet, we need a new account of reality. We need to know just who we are on the Earth, what Earth is, and what we are supposed to be doing here.

Our ideas form a system, with some beliefs more central than others. I shall single out the linchpins, the most fundamental concepts which have come down to us, deeply buried in us, on the basis of which human life is going forth.

Jung, earlier in this century, claimed that all individuals participated in an inherited unconscious collective psyche of civilization. Our modern world did not come just "dropping from heaven." It has been formed through a long history, specifically, a long history of ideas—ideas about what human beings are, their place in nature, what nature is, etc. The ideas of great thinkers working alone in their studies have come down to us in the form of modern life, the shape of our civilization and its institutions, our values.

Western civilization has developed from two legacies, that of Athens and that of Jerusalem. It embodies certain fundamental beliefs about the nature of reality stemming from these two legacies. These ideas have consequences. They shape our lives, and our expectations. But now, in modern times, they can be more fundamentally evaluated, for their result—the result of living them out—is the destruction of the Earth. Essentially, we are destroying the planet on which we absolutely depend for survival, and with it, ourselves.

The crisis in Earth is really the negative result of an experiment. In a deep sense, the human race has been proceeding just like a scientist in his/her laboratory, on the basis of certain assumptions about the reality being studied, asking: are these ideas correct? We have only forgotten to pose this as a question. Now, the Earth is answering: No. We have to return to our system of beliefs, to reexamine our own fundamental premises, and to replace them with better ones. We need a new understanding of reality.

Plato called mind "the guardian of the soul." In the following pages, we shall unearth some of the mistaken beliefs of our culture, our civilization, on the basis of which we are destroying the planet and ourselves, and free ourselves from them.

Eastern ideas will scarcely be touched on. Ancient eastern traditions were in touch with the Earth, as were our own, but today eastern civilizations destroy the Earth as avidly as we do, on the basis of imported western ideas of science and technology, western ways of doing things.

Our century has been about beginnings and depths. Freud and Jung discovered the great depths of the human psyche, and how we are shaped by early childhood experiences, especially traumatic ones. Modern physics has explored the beginnings of the universe, and has a story about it, which purports to explain how we came to be, and it has discovered the great depths of space—a far cry from the Ptolemaic "ceiling" of planets and stars moving in great circles around us. The twentieth century is an explanatory century. Where we come from explains what we are. Nowadays, there is much emphasis on "telling our stories."

Freud was fatalistic, as is much of modern science. Where you come from determines what you are, forms you, molds you and makes for you your prison.

This is not so. Human beings are ever standing slightly beyond their first premises. We are formed by ideas, yes, but there is something in us which opposes ideas, thrusts against them, the life force. Some ideas we hold confine life, others help it to flourish, and we all know the wonderful liberty we experience when we let go of old ideas about ourselves, outgrow them, and find better ones.

Even Freud knew that to remember/recover/relive the old painful traumatic experiences of childhood was to heal one of their effects, to free one of bondage to them. So we are never fully the captives of our ideas. We are free to change. It is by means of the ladder of better, more adequate, more powerful ideas that we are enabled to climb out of the darkness of Plato's cave. Better ideas form for us the stairway out of darkness and into the light of day. The end of human life is healing and wholeness. There is no darkness in civilization, in culture or in our own beings, which the healing light of truth cannot penetrate.

What is the test of the adequacy of our ideas? Our own fullness of being, our well-being and greater being are critical measures. There is a deep connection between our ideas, what we have become, and the state of the planet.

Plato claimed that the philosopher, like a good butcher, must carve the bird of existence at the joints.

The crisis in Earth is telling us that it is time for a new classification of Being, one that takes Earth into account. Plato cites Socrates in *The Phaedrus* as saying: "From trees and animals I have nothing to learn, I learn from human beings." Really? Perhaps the crisis in Earth is telling us we have much to learn from trees and animals, if we learn the languages that they speak. It is time to heal our ancient memories, the unconscious yet binding chains formed by the past, and to free ourselves for life.

Such is the purpose of this work.

The decisive carving of reality in which the western tradition has unfolded was given by Plato. Whitehead called the whole of western philosophy "a series of footnotes to Plato." This carving, this classification, is embodied in Plato's "Allegory of the Cave."

Briefly: Human beings dwell in an underground cave, chained by their necks so they can only see the wall in front of them. There is a fire behind them, and men and animals pass to and fro, the fire casting their shadows on the wall. The chained inhabitants take these shadows to be reality, and compete for prizes in measuring their behavior.

If someone were to come down into the cave, release the chains, and lead the inhabitants up the stairway and into the world above, they would at first be utterly dazzled by the light. Then gradually they would make out the shapes of trees, animals, and people, and finally see the sun itself, and understand what their condition in the cave truly was. But alas, no one ever comes down into the cave.

This fateful image of the human condition has been the backdrop against which the drama of philosophy has unfolded. The great tradition is ending in our time.

Heidegger, earlier in this century, called the entire philosophical tradition to account as "forgetfulness of being." We need a new classification, a whole new understanding of reality in which all the little labels and the incredible verbiage of our society may disappear, yielding to a new rich silence, and a being and beholding of all that truly is. It's all a question, in the terminology of modern times, of knowing something about the right brain, of connecting the left brain with the right, and of assimilating what the young are up to.

Essentially, I am proposing that we turn to an Earth centered perspective, and that all the great questions of human life, nature and destiny be referred to Earth as a touchstone for human theories and ways of life.

Plato referred to the metaphysician as the "physician of the soul." Nowadays, few know they have a soul. So it is as a physician, employing the art of medicine, rather than as a mathematician or a physicist bound by the rigors of deduction, that I shall proceed. The human heart-soul is my concern, and I shall care for it by addressing the human mind. Our ideas make us what we are. My hope is that I open the way for others to come after me, better physicians, with keener diagnostic tools and more effective remedies.

Perhaps the question, "How should we live?" is the only real question for us all. When we know what reality is, and who we are, then we will know how to live. Our century has given us beginnings and depths. What is now in question is the lived life. That is our horizon. What can we be, here? How can we live on this beautiful blue-green Earth?

I shall propose that the universe and ourselves are more glorious, and greater, and deeper, than anything we have ever imagined before. And I write, not for great men alone in their studies, nor philosophers in their academies, but for all who wonder—as all do—what human life is, what we are truly about here. I try to make my findings accessible to everyone.

Let me, then, reenchant us with our universe, through the

telling of certain stories old and new, by holding up ideas which shall function as giant lenses through which to see things in new ways.

At the outset, I wish to acknowledge my debt to Tom Berry, who was prophet for the Earth when no one else was paying attention to her. His writings are just now beginning to appear (*The Dream of the Earth, The Universe Story*). Our paths differ somewhat, but Tom, now almost eighty, has been my inspiration, and it is my hope that the whole story can now be put together in some fashion that makes sense of ourselves.

Here then, with due respect to Tom, is a work of the right brain speaking to the left. I offer a sketch of the true shape of things. If my lines are strong, that is because I would rather be presumptuous than evasive.

Here, then, is a woman's version of being.

IDEAS AND PRACTICES

Healing Our Minds and Our Planet

Ideas are the most dangerous things, they make us what we are.

—Ludwig Edelstein

The Significance of the Earth for Metaphysics

The Agony of the Earth

The Earth is in agony. In Brazil, her rain forest is being burned to provide land for settlers, land so infertile that it can be farmed for only two or three years, and then more forest must be burned. She is losing an area of rain forest larger than Nova Scotia every year. And with the forest go whole, unknown species of plants and animals. It is estimated that we lose a species every half hour.

In Ethiopia, the forest has been cut, the land is wasted and blowing away. In the rest of Africa, forest is disappearing to make room for farmland, and with it are going magnificent animals. Because of soil erosion, deserts are increasing over the whole Earth, and the climate is changing everywhere.

The ozone layer of the upper atmosphere is disappearing, permitting harmful radiation to destroy organisms at the base of the food chain.

Lakes, rivers and oceans are polluted, animals and plants are dying, pesticides and herbicides are now thought to form a thin layer over the whole of North America.

Why is all this happening?

Because of us. We human beings are the cause of the agony of the Earth.

The destruction of the Earth is the result of the most costly life-style the world has ever seen. We have developed a society devoted to making money by degrading high-energy resources of the Earth into unusable junk. The crisis in the Earth is directly caused by the affluent nations. Why are Africans cutting down the trees and destroying precious animal habitat? Because otherwise they have no cooking fuel. Why is Brazil cutting down the rain forest? To pay back foreign debts. Why are the Ethiopians starving? Because land which could grow staple crops for the people is being used to provide luxury items for the west. We here in North America, in Europe and Japan, are the real cause of the agony of the Earth. Because we voraciously amass and consume limited goods; because we do not limit our appetites on a planet which has limits; because we do not share.

I do not need to document the crisis further here. The United Nations report on the environment appeared a few years ago. Every day our newspapers and magazines convey news of fresh disasters. We have caused a crisis to Earth's living systems so that now the very survival of our 5 billion-year-old planet is in question. All this, in a cosmic instant.

What does the crisis in the Earth tell us about ourselves? Not just that we are greedy and destructive, not just that we do not know our proper place or function on Earth. It tells us that many of our ideas, our conceptions of reality, are false.

For human beings are the most peculiar animals. We live by powerful ideas—ideas about God, the universe, the Earth and ourselves—ideas which are like giant lenses through which we look at the world around us. These ideas are not always explicit, but are often deeply buried assumptions on which our lives proceed. If we want to change our ways, we have to bring them up into the light of day.

The crisis in the Earth calls into question the civilization which is bent on destroying its own life support systems. And it also calls into question the major ideas on which that civilization is built. For, at the heart of our way of life, hidden behind all the concrete and glass, is a framework of ideas around which modern civilization is structured. It is a law of logic that if p implies q, it is the case that not-q, then, is not-p. The crisis in the Earth tells us that our major ideas about God, the universe, ourselves and the Earth, and the civilization based on them, are false. We have an inadequate conception of our place in the scheme of things. If we and the Earth are to survive, if our civilization is to change, we have to do some fast, hard thinking.

The crisis in the Earth is a crisis of attitudes and values. More deeply, it is a crisis of ideas. Since all things are interrelated, it reflects the fact that the human race today is without an adequate understanding of Reality. It is without a metaphysics.

We need a new vision of the universe, a new vision of Reality and our place in the scheme of things. Just what is the Earth? Who are we? What are we supposed to be doing here? We have allowed the advertisers to answer these questions for us. Now we must take them into our own hands.

Metaphysics

The term "metaphysics" suggests something to do with the soul for New Age people. But metaphysics has a long and rich history in the west. The term itself derives from a work of Aristotle which was placed after physics by an early scholar, and which turns out to be a more inclusive account of reality than that provided by the physics. It contains talk about God and the laws of thought as well.

Throughout the ages, metaphysics has become associated with a baggage of terms which mainly derive from Aristotle and the scholastics—essence, form, matter, substance. But more deeply, it has always meant theory of reality, of ultimate reality. Of what's really real.

In our time, it is primarily scientists who are doing metaphysics in this second sense. Modern science is the major interpreter of the nature of reality in the twentieth century, and has cast all other disciplines into its shadow. Modern science has a dazzling account of the cosmos which rivals the great Gothic synthesis of the Middle Ages.

But the terms of modern science, which originated in the Greek fascination with geometry, and found firm footing with Descartes' cleavage of all of being into mind and matter, now drain all the joy from our lives. Science provides us with comfort, with the security of technology, but for the most part it leaves the spirit cold. As Brian Swimme put it, "It is driving us all insane."

It is time, once again, for metaphysics in Aristotle's sense as "that which comes after physics, and is the more inclusive account." Heidegger called human beings "the animal metaphysicuum." *All* human beings pose ultimate questions to themselves, but most are now intimidated by the enormous and complex systems of knowledge we have raised about us which are crushing us, and by the "experts" in all fields who are eager to advise us on how to live our lives.

For the most part, I am not. I live a wilderness life, marginal to the complexities of modern life. Wilderness life cleanses the mind, and enables one to gain some perspective on civilization. I have been an explorer and a dreamer here, a brooder of mysteries, a lover of frontiers. I put myself wholly with God because I wanted to write metaphysics and I knew that God alone could make it possible. "By Thy sweet scents draw me." This had been my dream since the age of twenty-one. When it all came together for me, in my forty-eighth year, even I was surprised by its form.

Plato thought the highest philosophy and that which most delights us was "the play of Reason." Philosophy has not been playful for centuries. It has been done by serious-minded men in academies. I live in a log house in the woods, surrounded by flowing streams, engaged in a thousand practical tasks, visited occasionally by moose and deer. I know something that the great men don't know.

And so, I propose in these pages to write metaphysics once again, as "what comes after physics," as a whole new theory of Reality, and as our highest form of play, for we are the creature who laughs. I will write it in terms everyone can understand, in the company of our first and great teacher here, the Earth.

Science tells us all about the Earth, as matter, as mechanism. This account is extremely impoverished and limited, despite its apparent richness, and it will be called into question, together with all our previous traditions and their categories. We shall move beyond them to include and overcome them in a new synthesis. The last three hundred years have been a spiritual desert, culminating in a technological civilization which ravages the Earth. Let us hope the next three hundred years may see the regeneration of both the human and the planet.

Directions

I can vividly remember sitting on the steps of my small cabin late one day last December. The sun was just setting over the hills which faced me across the valley, and all the air was still save for the crackling of frozen twigs and the creaking of the dark spruce as they swayed gently in the cold. The land was covered in snow.

I sat for an hour or so, communing with the silence. Later that night, the moon was full and we took a walk down the moonlit trail. Deer bounded ahead of us on the packed skidoo path, we could hear coyotes howling in the distance, owls swooped from tree to tree above us. All this is magic to my child's heart. When I returned out of the dark and mysterious woods, filled with light and shadow, my soul was full, for I had been in the presence of God.

The Earth is beautiful, and beauty is, as Plato knew, the one form which shines "here" as it does "there."

Nothing puts us so quickly in touch with God as does beauty, and the awe and reverence which beauty awakens in us. Beauty was, for the psalmists, God's most visible attribute.

The beauty I live with daily in the wilderness, the beauty of the living, breathing, awake Earth, her winds, her solitudes, her silences, her raging winter storms—and the health and wholeness which derives from having to adapt to *her* necessities—have brought me into the beginnings of knowledge of the Earth, and of the living God who dwells in her, felt as a mysterious presence.

For there is time in a wilderness life, time to be deep in one's own soul, time to be with oneself in doing a myriad of practical tasks, time to listen to the wind and to commune with a tree, time to sense one's body, the working of one's mind, where a word comes from, to see just how an egg sits and how a hammer hits, these profoundest of mysteries hidden by modern ways of "explaining the world." There is time to learn the ways of the Spirit, the Tao.

The city is a different world. It is a mystical world, to those with eyes to see; one meets Christ daily in the city streets. But it is a limited world, a ghetto in which humanity hides itself from the real universe, an artificial, fabricated world, bound by convention rather than the natural, in which no one can truly be oneself, living the day in accord with the flow of one's own energies. One must shut down one's senses to live in a city. City people have time for very little, sometimes not even for dinner, that sacrament of the day. The air is full of what Chief Seattle called "the clatter and noise of white man's cities," and one can scarcely hear one's own thoughts. Bound by the nine-to-five schedule, no one is able to attune to one's own natural rhythms. Life is *talk*—about the latest news, the fashions, the issues of the day. No one has time to see or feel the Earth.

Our western life-style, in its present form, is costing the life of the Earth, yet for the most part, modern people do not realize the connection between the life-style to which they have become accustomed and the ecological disasters they read about in the papers, which are happening somewhere beyond the city gates. I doubt whether most feel any kinship with the Earth at all, for our western traditions have separated us from the Earth, and in our cities we can hide from the damage we are doing. The Earth has been, since Descartes, "mere matter," something to be analyzed and dissected in laboratories, a setting for drives and picnics, a bundle of mechanisms, a thing, a resource, a commodity to be bought and sold at will, to be used as we see fit. It is well to remember that we do not dissect our pets.

I believe we can no longer see the Earth because of the ideas in our minds about just what the Earth is, which are coming to us from past tradition. Much is now known about the power of our concepts to keep reality out. We are doing in the Earth on the basis of false ideas about her.

Someone has called modern civilization "the grave of failed utopias." Deeply buried in the modern world are a whole interlocking nexus of related ideas—about God, ourselves, the universe, the Earth, and how we are supposed to be. Human beings find identity where these ideas intersect today, as Age is passing away before us, and with them, its answers to these questions. We are ready for a fresh approach.

The centuries before us have been patriarchal centuries, dominated by mind, reason, and the masculine. Jung described the masculine principle as Logos: abstract, aggressive, assertive, judgmental, argumentative, logical, non-relational. This is the principle which has elaborated the modern world, and enshrined thinking and the worship of mind as one of our most important values. This tradition is ending in our time, and the male principle, full at the beginning, has grown thin and bare as the feminine energies flow into the planet. The male energies arrived at strength by suppressing and dominating the female; now it is time for the female energies, which were once strong on this planet, to rise up and unite with the male.

Just what is the feminine? Woman's essential principle Jung described as Eros: affirming, accepting, imaginative, poetic, relational, non-judgmental, loving, just what a technological civilization needs right now, just what the Earth needs.

I do not mean to hypostatize this distinction between the masculine and the feminine. It is the modern reflection of the older Yin/Yang distinction, or the difference between right and left brains. Actual men and women are mixtures, and strong women have firm animus backbones. But having taught in a Great Books school, where every book except one was written by a man, and these were primarily taught by men, I know there is something valid about this distinction. I use it to contrast the sterile civilization we have fabricated in modern times, with what could be.

Patriarchy is ending in our time. What would a world woven by women look like? What would metaphysics, written by a woman, look like? It is time to raise once again all our most ultimate questions in the context of the crisis in the Earth. We are at a major historical turning point. If we do not change our ways now, if we do not change our mind-set, the Earth and ourselves may well disappear into the darkness of space.

So just when we think we had everything settled, we must

raise, once again, the most fundamental of all questions: Who are we? What are we meant to be doing here? What and where is God? How are we to live on the organic Earth?

Diagnosis

Tom Berry is convinced that our present historical task is to mediate the human–Earth relationship. He has recently urged us to *commune* with the Earth. "We must learn to commune with the Earth or we will do her in." Nowadays, our minds are fettered by a legacy of ideas which makes such communion impossible. The ideas of Descartes are the most serious.

Briefly, in the seventeenth century Descartes classified the whole of Reality into two "substances," mind and matter. God and human beings alone had mind, everything else—the Earth and all her inhabitants—was matter. This classification of being was a masterstroke for developing science, but it stripped the anima from Earth, reducing Earth to "that which has weight and is extended in space." It is rumored that Descartes' followers went about kicking dogs, just to hear them howl, reckoning the howls due to the wiring of the machinery, not to any inner feelings of pain. So Descartes separated human beings from the Earth, and we have been deeply separated ever since.

Modern science has a new evolutionary account of creation which makes human beings a part of Earth, connected with Earth, but it has introduced new problems. Science has discarded mind altogether in favor of the brain, and the universe is considered to be a vast sea of matter without mind. That includes human beings. Our world today is the consequence of believing there is "only matter." No wonder our life is for the most part melancholy monotony and many of us die tired of it.

But Descartes is only making fully explicit an essential distinction enshrined in the tradition before him. Our hatred of the Earth, our destructive attitude to the Earth, originates in the creation stories which come to us from both Athens and Jerusalem.

If scripture is the word of God, it is the word as interpreted by human beings, specifically, male human beings. The words of Genesis tell us that "human beings are made in the image of God" (no other creature is), and that "we are to have dominion over the Earth and subdue it." These notions, underpinning the entire tradition of thought before us, have, in this century, permitted the greatest possible plundering of the planet. The crisis in the Earth calls all notions which have brought about this crisis into question. The whole religious and philosophical tradition of the Piscean age can be looked at as the fearful unravelling of the implication of our creation stories.

In the Genesis story, God forms the Earth from without, as a potter makes a pot. God is not in the pot, the pot is not Divine, and we are free to explore it as we wish.

In the *Timaeus* account of Plato, the Demiurge has limited powers. He does not create matter, he merely finds this unruly stuff lying about and "persuades" it to form a cosmos. Matter is always getting out of hand, the cause of all unreasonable disasters. Plato wondered whether there was a form for such a thing as mud, and Aristotle referred to matter contemptuously as "hyle."

In ancient times Earth was worshipped as a goddess, but our patriarchal creation stories placed God outside creation, and Earth began to lose her divinity. It makes a difference whether you consider Earth divine or not. The Greeks had the blueprints for a technology which they never implemented because, in nature, they saw gods everywhere. But early scientists reasoned that God was like a watchmaker, God was not in the watch, God was divine, but not the Earth; hence, we were free to explore it at will. Jesus loved the Earth and found in her everywhere symbols for the spiritual life—the grain of wheat, the flowers of the field—but patriarchal tradition has stripped her of her magic. With Descartes she was fully recognized as "matter," and we have accordingly done her in. You cannot commune with "mere matter," or bundles of mechanisms, a "thing." The dualisms which lace the Piscean Age—body/soul, Earth/heaven, matter/mind—all originated with our creation stories, and they always place Earth in the shadows.

Here we are in modern times, "post-modern," as they are called. The intellectual world has completed a long deconstruction of previous tradition and is exhausted, locked into skepticism whose boat, as Kant put it, "lies on the shore and rots." Descartes is the culprit, but no one knows just what to do about him. If he had taken philosophically the rich dreams by which he guided his life, we would now be living in a different world. As it is, Descartes is deeply the founder of modern civilization.

We are beginning to recognize the reality of the Earth, to realize that she is a fragile ecosystem on whom we are utterly and totally dependent for life. But the human species, outgrowing all its natural checks and balances, thanks to the intervention of modern science, like a cancer is consuming its own host. Out of communion with the Earth, we are destroying her.

This is the context in which we shall write metaphysics.

New Beginnings

My last name is Green. Green is the color of hope in the Catholic tradition, and the last thing remaining in Pandora's box after all the nasties have been let out.

So I wish to offer a metaphysics of hope. The metaphysician believes that it is time to make a new beginning, a new departure in thought, that all about us are the harbingers of dawn. The owl of Minerva has flown at the end of one historical day, and is turning into the cock who crows at the outset of another.

At present we are the victims of economists and advertisers. Catholics, Protestants and all religions are linked, not by the sharing of a common founder, but in being consumers of the planet. This is because all religious traditions, without religious experience, have grown thin and bare and we have no sound metaphysics to put against the idolatries of our day. Because we have no metaphysics, modern human beings lack identity. The question of who we really are, of human identity, is the twentieth-century question.

Who are we, then? We cannot answer this question without making decisions about the nature of the reality in which we find ourselves. So, let us begin metaphysics. We shall take what is best in our traditions, and reconcile them with the Earth, and with the new positive ideas just now emerging. We shall begin at the beginning, with the new story of the cosmos, elaborated by modern science.

In the course of this work, we shall rewrite the fundamental premises of Descartes, the science that is based on them, and the theology that made them possible. We shall come to a new view of God, the universe, ourselves and the Earth from a base of some of the best teachings of Catholicism, but greatly expand them beyond the present teachings of the church, for it is time for a new development in the human consciousness.

I took up wilderness life at the age of forty-one, because I wanted, like Heidegger, to distance myself from cities to come to a place where language was simple and basic. In wilderness life, I brooded over the great traditions—science, philosophy, religion—against the realities of the Earth. It finally all came together when I was forty-eight, and I returned to Toronto to find out "where civilization was at."

Here is the essential way I understood reality when I was twenty-one, before I took up traditions of patriarchal thought. It has taken me this long to be able to make what was implicit then, explicit. (Yes, and many years of inner healing as well.) I ask you to take it as a gift from my path, which has led me from universities and great cities into a wilderness life, to yours. I will simply say in a straightforward way what I now see. I sought for truth a very long time and now "my spirit exults in God my savior." I am intoxicated by the true nature of reality, and what it means for us.

So I will tell the new creation story of modern science. But we need to turn to the roots of that science if we are to evaluate its story correctly. So let us begin, before the beginnings of the universe, with the beginnings of science. As Archimedes said: "Give me a place to stand, and I will move the world."

The New Story of Modern Physics

Classical Science

The Greek world was described by Ptolemy: the Earth was at the center of the universe, the planets and the sun travelled around it in great circles, and the fixed stars formed a comfortable ceiling. Human beings were at the very center of the universe, and everything they did was important.

Copernicus changed all this by discovering that the sun, not the Earth, was the center of the solar system. When his findings were published, there was a rash of suicides in Europe, for people concluded that if this were so, then all values must be "merely relative."

Following Descartes' classification of reality into mind and matter, which stripped of matter all that would be difficult to deal with and left it just as that which "has weight and is extended in space and time," Newton elaborated the great mechanical vision of the world. Newton, inspired by Greek geometry, applied number to the visible world. $F = ma$—force on a body is equal to the mass times the acceleration of the body. Laplace, following Newton, built a mechanical model of the solar system. When he showed it to the emperor, Napoleon, and Napoleon asked, "But where is God?" Laplace answered: "Sire, I have no need of that hypothesis."

God, who had been for ancient Hebrews as real as the Earth, became, for modern science, a hypothesis to be discarded. The classical view of the universe was that it was like a great machine, formed of atoms which resembled billiard balls, bouncing off one another in the void, devoid of purpose, devoid of beginning or end. The universe most of us carry in our minds still is a bit like this.

Descartes had mind and matter, God and human beings had mind. Advances in physics got rid of God. Modern science is abandoning mind altogether in favor of the brain. In effect, we all live—uneasily—within materialism. The universe, including ourselves, is a vast sea of matter.

The past three hundred years of patriarchal "splits and separations" have been some of the most spiritually agonizing for the human race, because this classical picture of the universe is hostile to the human soul and fascinates only those enchanted by number and mechanics. Religious people have separated themselves completely from developing science, and the classical theories of matter have driven a wedge between scientific and religious camps.

Be not dismayed—modern matter has changed its nature. Far from being inert billiard balls, modern matter is made up of millions of small particles, dancing parts filled with energy and light, and the universe, although formed of mechanisms, is a much more complex "machine" than it was for Newton. One physicist likened it to a vast thought rather than a vast machine. Matter is beginning to look like the sort of thing God could come to us "through."

To make a long story short, as scientific experimentation went forward on the basis of Newtonian principles, it encountered stranger and stranger anomalies, until finally the clear outlines of the classical picture were disturbingly blurred.

It happened, appropriately enough—let there be light!— over the nature of light. Light shows itself as having the properties of either a wave or a particle depending on the experimental setup.

Along came Einstein. Einstein returned to Newton's assumptions, revised some of them, and proposed a whole new vision of the universe. To simple three-dimensional Euclidean space Einstein added a fourth dimension, time, and the theory of relativity was born, in which time-space form a continuum.

Human beings have gone, in a mere 2000 years, from a compact little world with ourselves at the center, to a vast material universe spread out, perhaps, to infinity, in which human beings would seem to have very little significance indeed.

So where are we in all of this?

We live on a rather ordinary planet around an average star at a far and insignificant corner of an immense galaxy containing billions of stars—some much bigger and brighter than ours—in a universe containing billions of such galaxies. No wonder the existentialists, our last philosophers, despair. How can we matter in all of this? If the universe still has a center, it is not here.

But we do matter and every one of us knows that somehow, in some way, we have some importance in all this.

The Delphic oracle told Socrates what was essential: Know Thyself. The twentieth century is the century of the story. We know one another by sharing our stories. So, a good story about the universe might situate the Earth in its greater context, and reveal our place in the scheme of things. It is a way to find out who we are.

Modern physics has a story about the universe which replaces ancient tales of gods and heroes. It is widely called "the new story" and I shall present it here. We shall ask whether it is a good story, a true story, the right story to empower vision for the earth. Let us begin at the beginning.

The New Story

According to the new story, the universe originated in a gigantic explosion—the "big bang"—some twenty billion years ago, a primeval fireball in which the universe expanded from "nothing" to twenty-six trillion miles across in three seconds.

In that explosion, all the elements of matter formed, complex forms emerging from simple ones, radiating outwards, condensing, coalescing, aggregating to form stars, planets, galaxies. The time for the process of formation of the universe was billions of years, a number so great as to be impossible to think about.

Earth evolved as a planet about the sun some five billion years ago. For millions of years, it lay desolate. Then, about three billion years ago, life emerged in the early seas. By slow processes of evolution, simple forms of life evolved in all shapes and sizes—single-celled beings, multicellular beings, sponges, jellyfish, worms, snails, tunicates. Early evolution was in the sea. But the Earth is inventive—with kidneys, lungs, backbones, the fish appeared. And from a fish-like ancestor, reptiles migrated onto the land, birds began to fill the air, and small mammals appeared, together with plants which formed the atmosphere, permitting all other forms to live. The time taken was billions of years, allowing all the emergent species to become a well-established and interconnected ecosystem of diverse populations.

The human came last, at eleven seconds to midnight on the plot of evolution into a single day. We are the newest, the youngest animal in all creation, the one who does not yet know how to fit itself into the interconnected whole. We are the animal who does not yet know its "place." We are too young to know truly who we are, or to be what we truly are.

The human arrived here roughly two million years ago. In the beginning, we lived in caves, hunting and gathering, our "tribal-shamanic" period.

Later, we discovered agriculture. This momentous event enabled us to settle down, to found villages, and later, cities. We began to manufacture, barter and trade, economics was born, and luxury, which inflames the state. In the beginning, our languages must have been simple, but they have become increasingly complex as our way of life has become complex.

The rise of cities brought people together, kept them in one place and made culture possible. Then came the great ages of the written word, the ages of Aries and Pisces, the religious and philosophical systems. With them flourished the arts, music, painting, drama. This aspect of human identity is the one we are most familiar with the last few thousand years.

So we come to the present age, the scientific-technological age, the industrial revolution, the modern worldviews of physics.

Such is the modern story of the coming to be of the universe, the Earth and ourselves. It is a mystery story, for some of the major questions have yet to be answered.

Human beings are metaphysical. They are the creatures that

must form a view of the world, and live in that world on the basis of that view. We have been living in the world, forming our world, on the basis of previous metaphysics which reduce the Earth to "matter," on the premise that the Earth is there for our benefit, to do with as we see fit, and that we, arriving last, must have been the goal of the whole process.

The crisis in Earth is telling us these notions are false. We need a whole new vision of reality.

Let us delve into our mystery story with a few questions. First, what came before the big bang, the primeval explosion? Where does the universe come from? Second, how did it happen? What is the explanation of this event? Third, is there some purpose for all this, some end to be achieved? Where is it all going? Fourth, for us who are so full of little purposes and plans, our eyes always on the clock, the immense age of the universe is overwhelming—twenty billion years! We are mere specks in the picture. How can we have any significance whatsoever?

Finally, what are we meant to be doing here on Earth? Christ has long been taken as the model, in the west, for who we are to be. But Christ? "The foxes have lairs, the birds of the field have their nests, but the Son of Man has nowhere to lay his head."

The facts astound and perplex us, yet our hearts sense that we do have importance, meaning, significance. Now we must begin to make explicit these intuitions of the heart by delving into the implications and the explanatory principles of the new story.

Deeper Meanings

The new story tells us three important facts about the universe. First, the universe is time-developmental. We must thus replace the previous spatially oriented metaphysics with a dynamic account. To be time-developmental means that the universe grows like an embryo, whole from beginning to "end," each part related to every other part. Later events are made possible by what happens earlier. All the later stages are somehow contained in the potentials of the beginning. The entire universe is contained in the nature of the atom, the richer reality.

Second, the universe is emergent. Later stages build upon, and incorporate, earlier ones.

Third, the universe has a history, and that history is contained in the modern-day universe for those who have eyes to see, just as the behavior of the modern human being and its world manifest the previous history of thought.

What does this story tell us about ourselves?

First, it emphasizes our continuity with the atoms, with inanimate matter, with all living forms—the animals and plants which have preceded us. We are genetically related to them. We have emerged through them. Our basic life structures, our protoplasm, our cells, our needs, our development, are the same. "Ontogeny recapitulates phylogeny" used to be a biological maxim. That is, in our development, we recapitulate all the major species' different forms.

We, like the animals and plants, carry the ancient seas in our bloodstreams; our hearts beat according to ancient rhythms; night and day, the sun and the moon continue to govern our lives as they govern those of the plants and animals. Like all our forbearers, we eat the fruits and vegetables of the earth in order to survive. Far from being "separate" from the Earth, we are continuous with all creation.

To put this another way: We are the first cousins of every creature on the planet. We need never feel alone here. We are earthlings. In our endeavor to fly to the stars, we have all forgotten this. We are earthlings, in and of Earth, aspects of Earth, a creative Earth. Earth invented carbon backbones, then put oxygen, nitrogen and hydrogen with them to see what they would do, invented cells, photosynthesis. The whole process of evolution is the creative work of the Earth. Earth came first, we came second; Earth is the primary reality, we are derivative. That is why I have capitalized the word "Earth." We are aspects of Earth. In us, Earth lives, breathes, thinks, moves, loves, and has its being.

Second, this story emphasizes the interrelatedness, the connectedness of every creature with every other creature. In the long process of evolution, each creature has found its way into a dynamic balance with all the creatures which came before it. Evolution had made of Earth a balanced ecosystem. Not the human alone, but the whole interconnected array, in all its variety of form and behavior, is the goal of evolution.

Therefore we destroy species at our peril. All of us exist in delicate webs of relationships, subtle and intricate pathways of dynamic balance, cycles of energy consumption and production. Destroy one creature, remove one link in the chain, and the whole fabric of life is damaged. We depend upon the well-being of the whole.

Third, the new story emphasizes our dependence on the Earth. We belong to Earth, we belong here, but we have forgotten who we are, and how to see. Earth is our only home. In order to appreciate Earth, we should all be compelled to live on the moon for awhile. Far from being "lords of the planet" we are absolutely dependent on her for every aspect of our lives, in a true master–slave relationship in which Earth is the master.

The philosophers have separated "life" from "spirit," mirroring the separation between women and men. Life, of course, is the inferior category, and flying to the moon, in all its aridity, just one more manifestation of spirit.

We are earthlings. For earthlings, life and spirit are one. This is just the first of many identities to be made in seeking answers to our fundamental questions.

Who are we then, in the vast complex of rivers, lakes and streams, mountains and hills, flourishing jungles and desert landscapes, animal and plant life? Who are we, huddled here in our cities, shielding ourselves from the cosmos around us?

We are the creature who has the word, in every way. We are creatures who live and function through a complex language. We thus relate to Being, not directly, but through the agency of the meanings of words. We live in a world mediated to us by meaning. That intervention means a certain alienation from that world. So Heidegger, a German philosopher of the first half of the twentieth century, called the entire tradition of western philosophy: "forgetfulness of Being."

We are the creature who seeks truth. That is the accord of our language structures, our theories, our ideas, with reality. We are always framing theories of what our world is, what Being is, what people are, which we hope in some way corresponds with or maps onto the real nature of things. We are always trying to see just where we are in the scheme of things, the true function of philosophy.

And then, we are the creature who, at least in an obvious way, worships. From the time of our earliest appearance, we worshipped—the forces of nature, gods, the Goddess, God. Now we worship the things of our own invention—computers, rockets, weapons.

We worship. There is a deep impulse in us to worship, to adore, to celebrate. There is an energy in us purely for praise. Today this energy is dammed up and stifled in us, because we do not know the what or the how of it, nor indeed whether there be anything to celebrate.

The answers to our questions will come. But we must now delve more deeply into the nature of the universe we live in. The story of our emergence has been told. Now, we have to fathom that story. We have to seek out its explanatory principles.

Tom Berry's Twelve Principles

Do we have the full account? Tom Berry has taken the new story of science seriously, has put forth twelve principles based on it for understanding the universe (see pages 36–37).

We need to single out, and consider in depth, only one of these principles, principle #3: "From its beginning, the universe is a psychic as well as a physical reality."

"Psychic and physical." By considering deeply the "conditions of the possibility of this dualistic phenomenon," we shall begin to fathom the true dimensions of the new story and its meaning for us.

According to the account of most modern scientists, the universe came to be by accident, by processes which Plato, who was familiar with scientific ways of thinking, called "chance and necessity." That is to say, by some "accident" in space and

TWELVE PRINCIPLES:

For Understanding the Universe and the Role of the Human in the Universe Process by Thomas Berry

1. The universe, the solar system, and the planet earth in themselves and in their evolutionary emergence constitute for the human community the primary revelation of that ultimate mystery whence all things emerge into being.

2. The universe is a unity, an interacting and genetically-related community of beings bound together in an inseparable relationship in space and time. The unity of the planet earth is especially clear; each being of the planet is profoundly implicated in the existence and functioning of every other being of the planet.

3. From its beginning the universe is a psychic as well as a physical reality.

4. The three basic laws of the universe at all levels of reality are differentiation, subjectivity, and communion. These laws identify the reality, the values, and the directions in which the universe is proceeding.

5. The universe has a violent as well as a harmonious aspect, but it is consistently creative in the larger arc of its development.

6. The human is that being in whom the universe activates, reflects upon, and celebrates itself in conscious self-awareness.

7. The earth, within the solar system, is a self-emergent, self-propagating, self-nourishing, self-educating, self-governing, self-healing, self-fulfilling community. All particular life systems in their being, their sexuality, their nourishment, their education, their governing, their healing, their fulfillment, must integrate their functioning within this larger complex of mutually dependent earth systems.

8. The genetic coding process is the process through which the world of the living articulates itself in its being and its activities. The great wonder is the creative interaction of the multiple codings among themselves.

9. At the human level, genetic coding mandates a further transgenetic cultural coding by which specifically human qualities find expression. Cultural coding is carried on by educational processes.

10. The emergent process of the universe is irreversible and non-repeatable in the existing world order. The movement from non-life to life on the planet earth is a one-time event. So too, the movement from life to the human form of consciousness. So also the transition from the earlier to the later forms of human culture.

11. The historical sequence of cultural periods can be identified as the tribal-shamanic period, the neolithic village period, the classical civilizational period, the scientific-technological period, and the emerging ecological period.

12. The main human task of the immediate future is to assist in activating the inter-communion of all the living and non-living components of the earth community in what can be considered the emerging ecological period of earth development.

time, atoms came into being having such-and-such properties. Because of these properties, which they acquired by chance, when they collide with other atoms, certain interactions "inevitably" come about, and certain stable combinations result.

Such is the "necessity" in nature. It is "mechanical" necessity, and the basis for forming a picture of a universe that is "running down." Even evolution, which would appear to be running uphill, is really just running down in a complex way.

In the scientific picture, the universe begins with atoms and molecules—"mere matter"—and ends with consciousness in us—"something that happens when matter reaches a certain degree of complexity."

But there is an ancient principle of both thought and being which suggests that you can't get out, at the end, what was not there in the beginning.

We have already surmised that the fireball—the atoms—must be the richer reality in that it contains all the possibilities of the universe in potential form. The emergence of the whole universe merely makes explicit possibilities already implicit in the beginning.

What does it mean to have a psychic dimension present from the beginning? How is it present? What scientific assumptions have to be rewritten in order to allow a psychic dimension to be present?

Modern science has given us the story. It has given the facts, but as yet the facts yield no meaning for us. But stories have meanings. They even have authors. We shall take some time to dig into its meaning for us, who come last and tell ourselves the story (hence, necessarily from a human-centered perspective), by determining whether the credentials of modern science fit it to be our final storyteller.

Now we must climb. We must climb up to first principles, and back to the beginning of things. We have to climb up past the maze of scientific categories for the world, to find out what the truth of science is.

So let us journey up the path of argument. The welfare of the Earth and of ourselves is at stake, as we grope for better accounts. As one well-acquainted with the sciences, let me give you in the following sections four major reasons why the sciences cannot be final storytellers. This, to prepare our way for metaphysics.

Limits of Science: The Unexplained Explainer

As a graduate student in science, I believed, like all my generation of scientists, that the truth was to be found down at the molecular levels of reality, and I headed down to the molecular frontier. When I arrived there, I was deeply disappointed. Not only did I not find truth, but I had lost the whole animal on the way down. I was in a sea of molecules without principles of differentiation.

I complained to my roommate about this, and she told me, prophetically: "Oh, you thought you'd find God among the molecules."

Well, if science had the complete picture of reality, shouldn't God have been there? Something was amiss. My classmates were satisfied with scientific accounts, but I was not. I began notebooks in which I pursued such questions as: What is explanation? What is it to explain something in terms of something else?

Night after night I sat in my little room in the library of Rockefeller University, watching tugboats ply the East River, pursuing my questions in notebooks. Now I want to share with you the substance of what I found.

The new story of the cosmos, as it stands, cannot be the story to empower the vision which humanity needs. It is taught to schoolchildren—nowadays everyone knows it—and greeted with neither wonder nor awe. It is just "more facts" to be learned. Something is amiss.

Tom Berry has done much to illuminate the story of the cosmos by simply drawing attention to certain implications of the facts of what is, by attending to the descriptive details of the story as it now stands.

He goes beyond present-day science in suggesting that the universe has a "psychic-spiritual" side as well as a material one. It is doubtful whether modern scientists would accept this claim. For modern science, the universe is just "matter" which, when it reaches a certain complexity in the human, produces "mind." The rest of the universe is a sophisticated machine.

If we are to interpret our place correctly in the scheme of things, it is this principle of Tom Berry's we must attend to. One of the reasons human beings feel so alienated from the rest of the universe is because they think they are the only ones that possess minds.

We cannot give a true account of the universe, the new story humanity has need of, until we prepare the way for the "psychic-spiritual" side of things. That way can only be prepared by challenging the claims of twentieth-century science to be the major interpreter of reality. For the secular world at large, science has this authority. But it is on the present-day scientific conception of Earth as a cleverly wired machine that Earth is being destroyed. The crisis in Earth demands that we find new and better concepts of her, and she gives us a mandate to examine all the fundamental assumptions on which we are proceeding. These are, in our time, the assumptions of science about the nature of reality.

What gives Tom Berry's cosmological thinking such freshness and such force is that he attends only to the scientific description of the process, the scientific account of just what happened. He does not so much concern himself with scientific explanations of the account. But the reason people are not especially enchanted by the new story is because of the scientific explanation given of it: chance events, necessary interaction, chance mutation and natural selection of the "fittest." We turn out to be the only beings in the whole universe with purposes, and we got here by accident.

It is the explanatory concepts of modern science which give it its tremendous hold over the human mind. Hence, we must grapple with them first, in order to indicate their limits, and with those limits, the limitations of modern science.

The criticism to be made is very simple: all scientific explanations rest ultimately on unexplained explainers, entities used to explain everything else, but which are not, themselves, understood. Key questions will make the meaning of this statement clear.

The heart speeds up in exercise. Why does it do this? Because adrenaline, secreted by the adrenal glands, is released in exercise and affects the permeability of the heart to certain ions which alter the rate of contraction.

Then we ask: how do the ions act to alter the rate? The answer would be something like this: the electrical charges on the ions combine with the fixed electrical charges on the contractile muscles in the cell, changing permeability, altering the rate of contraction.

We could then ask: how do the charges combine? The answer is that unlike charges attract, like charges repel.

Then we can ask: how do unlike charges attract? To this question no answer can be given or, if one appears, it will just push the question down an order of magnitude. At some point we run into a brick wall. No one knows how charges attract or repel. They just do. It is a "fact" of nature into which we have no insight.

Everything in science is explained in terms of the forces. What is a force? No one knows. In the absence of all knowledge, the term "force" suggests something mechanical: "pushes and pulls." The entire question of what is really happening is simply begged. Perhaps unlike charges attract for love or desire? There is no way to tell. As Tom Berry puts it: one atom knows what to do when it meets another.

Forces are the occult entities of modern science. No one knows what they are. But they are the fundamental terms in which the universe is today being explained. We cannot understand the universe without understanding their nature.

Modern science has this limit because science is always the spectator, the observer of "outsides," much as it appears to be in the very heart of nature, down among the molecules. In fact, science is tied to the nature it can sense (touch, see, smell) to nature as it lets us see it from the outside. We seldom realize this is what we are doing. Only at the innermost limits of explanation in an unexplained explainer does this standpoint show up.

What this means for us is that ultimately science cannot explain, it can only describe. We accept the scientific account of what happens, but not necessarily the scientific explanation. There may be much more going on within the universe than meets the scientific eye, and there may well be other ways in which to explore and know the universe than by the path of science.

Scientific explanation always rests on unexplained explainers, which are not, as Aristotle hoped the ultimate source of things would be, "transparent to intellect." On the contrary, they are utterly opaque. This fact, this unknowable interaction appearing at the basis of matter, must send a shaft of unknowability through the entire edifice of scientific knowledge. Order there is. How do we make that order intelligible? Explain it? A new story there is. What is the meaning of this story?

At this point, no one knows.

Limits of Science: Our Essential Selves Are Separable from Our Bodies

Now we question the whole edifice of scientific materialism.

Teilhard de Chardin, a scientist-philosopher-mystic living in the early part of this century, suggested that the universe has a "within."

Scientists have not been hospitable to the "within." They are only really forced to recognize it in the case of the human mind, which definitely seems to be an inner side of things. But then, they do away with it. Science after Descartes has discarded "ideas." It is the brain which does the work, ideas are just a by-product. As the philosopher William James put it: "The mind is to the brain as a shadow running along beside the runner, never influencing his stride."

But then, what are ideas doing there at all? If the patient being probed by the physiologist with electrodes had not told the physiologist that the inner correlate of the electrical activity on the oscilloscope was a whole train of beautiful thoughts, the physiologist would never have suspected the existence of ideas.

You will remember that science got its foothold by leaving human beings out of its account, and developing a vocabulary for matter—forces, momentum, mass, acceleration, volume, etc.

This is supposed to be an assumption-free, aseptic vocabulary with which to describe the natural world.

With the progress of science, human beings, too, have been assimilated into these categories. Thus, Freud described the psyche in terms of forces, and one hears much of social and economic forces. Human beings at the beach resemble the behavior of molecules at a liquid interface. The same kinds of long-range orders emerge at all levels of magnitude. Molecules and human beings appear to function according to similar laws.

So, materialistic science has assimilated human beings into the categories and concepts drawn up for matter.

The poet Rilke wrote that we are not at home in our interpreted world. What is unacceptable to human beings are just those categories and concepts. Does all come to be for "attraction and repulsion," or, in the terms of Empedocles, a pre-Socratic philosopher, "love and strife?" It makes a difference what language we use. Our terms are everything.

Human beings are not at ease in the scientific accounts of themselves. This may be a sign that something is wrong with those accounts.

All explanations rest on unexplained explainers. Now let us take a more decisive step to understanding what the universe is, in questioning materialistic principles in general. Let us turn to the explanation of mind.

A phenomenon is being explored at the frontiers of human experience/existence by doctors on cardiac wards. They call it n.d.e., near-death-experience, and it is made by patients with heart attacks, pronounced clinically dead (all vital signs ceased) and then resuscitated ten or fifteen minutes later.

Most of these patients describe experiences similar to those reported by Moody, in *Life After Life*. The far side of these experiences—glimpses into another reality—do not concern us here. What does concern us are the implications of the near side of these experiences.

Briefly, most resuscitated patients report the experience of finding themselves at some point hovering near the ceiling of the room, watching doctors work on their body below. In this state, they have complex thought processes about themselves, they observe readings on dials which would not be visible to them if they were lying in the bed, they describe exactly what procedures the doctors used to revive them. In short, they tie into all the necessary sense-data with which to make an out-of-body experience empirically verifiable by scientists. And then suddenly, just as their vital signs return, they wake up in the bed again. Such out-of-body experiences are being made, and observed by doctors, with increasing frequency. (See *The Near-Death Experience*, by Bruce Greyson and Charles Flynn.)

What do they mean for us? The universe is just beginning to lift its veil from its deepest mysteries. Out-of-body experiences (one was even made by the Nobel prize physicist, Richard Feynman, in a sensory deprivation tank) are familiar to the spiritual traditions of the world, but not to the scientific. They have great implications for the scientific account of reality, and they are our first move in bringing the two disparate traditions together.

In the first place, such experiences mean that we can see without eyes, hear without ears, and think without brains. That is to say, the essential human self is separable from the body, as the religious traditions have always insisted that it is.

In the second place, it means that at least one being in the universe—the human—has a non-physical as well as a physical side, and that hence, our pervasive materialism is a false doctrine, one of many false doctrines on the basis of which we are destroying Earth. No longer can scientists hold that there is only matter in the universe. The essential human self is non-material.

The question arises: How deep does the non-physical side of the universe go? Where do we come from? Whither do we go? And what about the animals, with whom we have an evolutionary continuity? And the atoms? Here is what Teilhard de Chardin called "the within" in us, and it is separable from the body.

Far-reaching speculations can be associated with this discovery which need not be considered here. They will appear later on. Suffice it to say that these out-of-body experiences made by so many, with essential evidence confirmed by doctors and scientists, are a kind of crucial experiment for the whole scientific explanatory schema. It is a significant challenge to scientific materialism, and opens the door to other interpretations of the universe.

It is quite possible that the human being, rather than being an embarrassing glitch in the system, is key to understanding the universe.

Limits of Science: We Are the Keys to the Universe

In this section, we shall make a major paradigm shift, the first of two to come in the course of this work. The universe is emergent. This means that later stages build upon, and incorporate, earlier stages. The universe is developmental.

The universe has unfolded out of the potentials of the big bang like a flower emerging from the ground. The first two leaves appear, out of these unfolds a stem, then more leaves. Do we know what this plant is yet? Is it finished? The bud opens, petals, stamens, pistil, and there is a glorious flower, a full plant complete in all its detail.

So this planet, dark by night, moonlit, blue-green by day, endlessly circled the sun. It lay fallow for ages, then brought forth life from its own creative processes. How slowly life unfolded, the potentials of carbon, hydrogen, nitrogen and oxygen, and then of a single cell. How slowly these potentials manifested themselves, struggled landward, riverward, skyward. Do we yet know quite what is happening? No. Millions of years pass—a very long time (the universe is patient). We do not yet know what this process is.

And then, human beings appear, the latest creature to be formed by evolutionary processes, the newest creature, the youngest, the most radically unfinished. Physical evolution may continue through it, it may not. Perhaps evolution will continue in some wholly different way, for the universe continues to unfold, and it unfolds through us.

Science evolved its categories of explanation by examining the early stages of the process and then, when we came along, it assimilated us to those early stages.

But we have a different status. We are like the flower of the plant. No one could have guessed that the plant had this potential until the flower bloomed. I want to suggest that we human beings, far from being forcibly fitted to a set of inadequate categories, are the keys to comprehending all that is hidden in the process. We are not more important than leaves and stems; we are different, and manifest a potential in their inner side we could not otherwise have known about. Teilhard de Chardin claimed that the universe had a "within." Indeed, it is just possible that all the formative powers of the universe lie in that "within."

Who are we, coming at the end of the process? We are the creature preoccupied with knowing the universe in laws and formulas, and in giving explanations of it.

We are also that creature in which we have an absolutely privileged standpoint in the universe. We do not merely gaze outwards, at nature. We look inwards, at our own inner life. In ourselves, and in ourselves alone, we have access to the "within" of the universe.

What does that mean? An emergent universe embodies the manifestation of two principles. First, the theory of evolution emphasizes our continuity with the rest of nature, and with the atoms and molecules, rather than our separation from it. By this principle of continuity (really, a new version of what St. Thomas Aquinas called the principle of analogy), we are just a privileged manifestation of what is in everything else.

The second ancient principle associated with emergence is that nothing is in the effect which was not first in the cause. We have to see the effect to know what was in the cause, but then we can see that the cause has the greater richness.

So, all the potentials of the human were present in the original fireball. The greatest and richest reality was present before the big bang, the second richest reality is present in the atoms just after. We are only manifesting properties present in the atoms.

This means that in ourselves we have access to the "within" of the whole material universe, and it may be in that within— disregarded by science—that the true formative powers of the universe reside. That within is, in ourselves, a psychic-spiritual dimension, and it may be such everywhere. Our two principles, "continuity," and "the cause richer than the effect," suggest that it is.

So, what do we find in ourselves? We find ideas and images. These are non-material things occurring in us. We know that we act on the basis of these ideas, ideas of what we want to do, of who we are going to see, of where we are going to go and of how we shall get there.

We know, in ourselves, ideals and imagination. We have visions of how we would like life and ourselves to be, visions of the future.

We know, in ourselves, a whole affective life of the emotions—hope, fear, exhilaration, joy, anxiety, despair, exuberance, love.

We know, in ourselves, when bundled up on a winter's day, or soaking up the sun, a most delicious sense of being-a-self. "I am-ness."

And we know, in ourselves, rich dreams welling up out of a night's sleep by which we can guide our lives.

Do other beings in the universe have all this too? Does the universe as a whole experience this? Are the great dark spaces around us really full of psychic inner life. Somehow, Yes.

Sooner or later, it dawns on most of us, in a flash of intuition, that all living beings are conscious. Perhaps we are not so sure about the atoms and molecules. But by our principle of continuity, the consciousness of living beings is derivative of the prior consciousness of atoms and molecules. The consciousness of atoms and molecules may be very different from the human, but consciousness nevertheless. The entire universe has a psychic-physical dimension, and we are the keys to understanding it.

Now the universe is beginning to look more interesting. It is not a machine, with interlocking parts. It is, quite possibly, conscious, and full of conscious beings. So, we dredge up our first, deep, by now unconscious for most, assumption, Descartes' distinction between mind and matter. He claimed that human beings alone had mind, everything else was matter. Scientists have reduced everything, including us, to matter. Now it would seem that in fact all material beings have mind. Descartes' distinction is one of standpoint—are we looking at them from the inside or the outside? Perhaps such a generalization as "all" seems a little excessive at this point. It will become more acceptable as we proceed.

Science still holds to its own explanatory principles, chance and necessity, the interplay of forces. It is thus in direct conflict with those who say the universe is intelligent and manifests design. This conflict of explanatory principles is the essence of the conflict between science and religion. How can this gap be bridged?

Earth demands that we be radical in our examination of scientific assumptions—and let us be clear that they are assumptions. Physics, which has always distinguished itself from religion, is in fact a religion, a set of rules, theories, laws, which determine the nature of acceptable reality. It is based on far-reaching assumptions which may have very little to do with the real nature of the universe. What lies beyond the religious structure is rejected. It is not even seen.

The major assumption of science is that matter precedes consciousness; consciousness appears only in us, and is second. My proposal is that it is just the other way around: consciousness precedes, that it is in all things, and only secondarily gives rise to matter and form. This is a Copernican inversion of the scientific position. It may better accommodate the emerging data.

What does this mean? Copernicus (1473–1543) worked with the Ptolemaic model of the universe, a model which assumed the Earth was the center of the universe, and explains the apparent motion of the planets around it by a complex series of circular motions, epicycles. Finally, the calculations were so complex that Copernicus decided to make a new and different assumption—that the sun, and not the Earth, was the true center of the universe, and that all planets, including the Earth, circled the sun. He made this change, redid the calculations, and discovered that he could account for the observations—save the appearances—with much simpler calculations. He rewrote the major assumptions of astronomy, and totally changed—and challenged—the world of his time.

It was the reasoning of Copernicus which helped to enshrine in science the notion that "the simplest" is best. This principle came later to be known as Occam's razor. Modern science, in disregarding ourselves and most of reality in order to simplify its starting point, shaves away half the face with the beard.

Similarly, Immanuel Kant (1724–1804) wrestled for many years with the fact that human reason, when speculating about God, freedom, immortality, had so little success and so little agreement among thinkers, whereas science seemed to be proceeding on a sure and a firm path, accepted and agreed upon by all who knew the experiments. Finally, it occurred to Kant to effect a "Copernican revolution" in thought. Instead of assuming, like Aristotle, that the mind was a blank slate which assumed its structure from the world, Kant made the assumption that the form of the world is provided by the knowing mind, which brings certain categories of its own to experience. The mind, and not the world, originates the way we perceive things. The world as-it-is-in-itself is unknowable to us. It is as though we are wearing purple glasses, so that everything looks purple. And for Kant, we can never take off the glasses.

What of the successes of science? Science is "empirically real" but "transcendentally ideal." That is to say, it knows the world as it appears to us, but not as it is in itself.

So, for many reasons, it would appear that the "classical" account of reality by science has become disturbingly blurred as new data are coming into the picture. Earth is giving us the mandate for change. The crisis in Earth, which is a function of our attitudes and life-styles, is really a challenge to the whole scientific way of looking at things. The many confirmed out-of-body experiences, familiar to spiritual traditions and now witnessed by doctors, challenge the fundamental explanatory principles of science.

Such a Copernican reversal/revision of fundamental assumptions may not at once help scientists in their laboratories, but it will have immediate practical implications for the rest of us, for the right living of our lives, for right attitudes and right relationship to Earth. As we take on the right understanding of Being—namely "consciousness precedes matter and form"—we will come to see the world in new ways, ways that lead us to entirely new questions altogether. For one thing, this means that the whole planet is animate.

Let us summarize all these suggestions concerning the new assumptions on which life must proceed:

1. All beings have a within. Even a potato has a within.
2. This within is a psychic-spiritual dimension in nature which we may call consciousness.
3. Consciousness precedes matter and form.
4. The true explanatory principles of the universe are to be found in consciousness.

All these principles mean that nature and the universe are more like us than we ever dreamed possible. We are surrounded by our own kind. Perhaps, now, we may begin to feel at home here, and to take up our relationship with the rest of the planet.

And there are further implications. If consciousness is first, and takes on matter and form, only to set it down again, perhaps consciousness does not perish. We know, in the human case, it is entirely separable from the body. Perhaps, indeed, there are eternal elements in the human condition as so many of us have suspected. And then, if the psychic-spiritual side of the universe is really the formative source of all we see, that is reason to say that the universe is spiritual rather than material.

Then the question arises: how deep does the psychic-spiritual go? We know that the human being can exist in separation from the body. The principle of plenitude—all possibilities which could be realized are being realized—suggests to us that there could be spiritual beings which never materialize. We have taken ourselves to be the lords of creation, the very goal of the evolutionary process. In fact, we may be at the very bottom of a spiritual hierarchy of non-embodied intelligent beings in comparison with whom we are mere beginners. This would be a salutary perspective from which to ask what we are supposed to be doing on the planet, a question meaningless from the scientific perspective, but now most meaningful indeed.

Finally, there is an implication for knowing. We may have many ways of knowing the universe other than those relied upon by science—the data of the senses. We are much bigger than the senses. We can hear, see and think without them. What other modes of knowing do we have?

How deeply is the universe like us, like our life of feeling, heart and soul?

These are tantalizing questions for understanding our place in the scheme of things, a source in us—after all these centuries of mechanism—of feeling we belong.

The Anthropic Principle

Perhaps we are beginning to feel that we belong here, that the universe is not hostile to us, nor we to it. Indeed, recent developments in physics suggest that the universe wants us to be here.

For centuries, scientists have assumed they were "going it alone." That by sheer dint of will and reasoning, they were wresting nature's secrets from her. But there are some curious facts which suggest this is not quite the case. In the first place, scientific reasoning goes only so far. Insights, when they come, are neither "willed" nor "wrested." They are "given." They flash into the scientist's mind unexpectedly, when he/she is walking through the woods or climbing a hill, or thinking of something else, or daydreaming. They come very much as a revelation from the depths.

Secondly, fundamental solutions to problems often occur to two or three people at the same time, as if there were a frontier of thought and the community of knowers were proceeding together into the deeper recesses of knowledge. It seems, somehow, that only when the human mind is well-prepared for it does the universe unveil its face.

Finally, always just when we think we have all the answers, as we thought we had everything sewed up with classical physics, the universe will spring a big surprise, forcing us to reexamine assumptions that now seem naive, and introduce us to a more profound conception of the world. Such was Einstein's transition from three-dimensional to four-dimensional space.

Lately, the surprises have become more and more astounding. Physicists at the frontiers of scientific investigation are beginning to have the uncanny sense that just as they are observing the universe, the universe is observing them. In brief, they are finding startling coincidences. Certain large numbers for phenomena which, on the face of things, seem quite unrelated, are the same.

Brian Swimme recently communicated some of the mysteries of physics (Colloquium of Holy Cross Centre, summer 1987). In the beginning, scientists recognized that the human mind had projected itself all over creation, so it stripped its fundamental terms absolutely bare in order to find out what was what. Nature, in their descriptions, was nothing but facts and arbitrary numbers. It is this bare language, this absence of meaning, which is driving us all insane, but that is the reason behind it. And the deep hope was that by stripping description bare, scientists would actually end up being closer to the real universe.

But now, a certain non-arbitrariness is showing up in the scientific descriptions. There are three numbers which Brian calls "sacred," in that if they were different, the universe would be completely different, if it existed at all.

The first is the number for the rate of expansion of the universe. The discovery of the expansion of the universe is one of the great discoveries of the twentieth century, and physicists now realize that the rate is just right. If it were a little faster, the whole universe would fly apart; if it were slower, the universe would collapse into itself due to gravitational forces. The actual rate means that gravitational and expansile forces are maintained in a delicate balance, and we have an orderly universe.

The second "sacred" number is that for the distance of the earth from the sun. Any closer, it would be too hot and its atmosphere would evaporate; any farther, and it would be too cold.

The third "sacred" number is the size of the Earth. If it were any smaller, gravitational forces would have predominated over electromagnetic ones, and the Earth would have stopped at rocks as has the moon; if it were any larger, it could not hold together and would end up gaseous like Jupiter. The size of the Earth—6,000 kilometers—just that point at which the gravitational and the electromagnetic forces balance.

What can we make of this? Could it all have happened "by accident?" But there are even more stunning surprises—an apparent non-arbitrariness of certain large numbers. Briefly, if one compares the electromagnetic with the gravitational force, it turns out to be 10^{40} times as strong. But then, the number of particles in the universe (this can be calculated) turns out to be 10^{40} squared. And as if that weren't enough, the time taken for the evolution of the universe from the beginning until now (measured as the interval taken for light to pass through an elementary particle) is 10^{40}.

Now what does all this mean? These astounding coincidences suggest some kind of deep order in the universe, some order whose meaning we do not understand.

Brian went further in an attempt to make sense of it all. He pointed out an even more interesting fact—two of these numbers are fixed, the ratio of the forces and the number of particles in the universe. But the third one, the time from origins to here, is not fixed. Only now, only at this very precise moment in time, could physicists be making this observation. In another one hundred years, no one could say this. What does this mean?

Admiration and awe for the mysteries of the universe are on the increase among physicists. As Brian Swimme put it: "It is as though the universe has been planning a big surprise party for us in which it will reveal just how magical it really is. It has been keeping us out the door until all is in readiness—is everyone here? . . . is the band ready? . . . the cake? Okay, let them in!"

Teleology is reappearing in modern science not, now, as "final cause," but as "coincidences," as identities.

This new sense of the universe, and the true nature of scientific investigation, has culminated in a recent book, *The Anthropic Cosmological Principle*, by J. Barrow and F. Tipler. This book takes up these themes. It reviews all the forms of teleological thinking (i.e., explaining natural events in terms of final causality, or purposes) up to the present. Many physicists, as mentioned in this book, now subscribe to the "anthropic principle." Put one way, this principle says: the universe was designed with us in mind. Put another way, the principle says: the universe has been expecting us.

What does this mean? It means, in the first place, that modern physicists are beginning to suspect "design" rather than "chance and necessity" in the coming-to-be of the universe. Scientists climbing up the mountain are meeting the theologians on their way down.

And secondly, and most important for us, it means that we human beings belong here. The universe has been expecting us, the universe cares about us. It means that the universe wants us, else we would not be here. And now it makes sense to ask the deep questions of the human heart: what is our place in the whole? What are we here for? What is the purpose of human existence in this rather far-off corner of a medium-sized galaxy, circling about a fairly average star?

The universe wants us. It wants us, and it wants Earth.

There is hope for us.

Knowing, Scientific and Otherwise

The tradition of knowing in western science and philosophy descends from Greek rationality, from the legacy of Athens. (The legacy of Jerusalem is revelation.)

For Plato, the paradigm of knowing was geometric knowledge. The axioms and definitions of geometry were true descriptions of the nature of an invisible and eternal reality, and from them, the being (summarized in the proofs) of every other element necessarily followed.

This geometric way of thinking has dominated both science and philosophy in the west, where argument is the prevalent mode, perhaps most fully realized in Spinoza's *Ethics*. For Plato, argument always ended in uncertainties, contradictions, *aporea*, which may be an indication that indeed, the world is part real, part appearance or camouflage.

For modern science, mathematics is not indubitable truth

about essential reality, but a construct (of which there are many), a tool, or even a language with which to describe reality; and modern physics does not really base itself on the geometric model of reality which has for so long dominated the western imagination but, as Fritjof Kapra has shown so clearly in *The Tao of Physics,* shares the fundamental conceptual structure of eastern mysticism. Science and the procedures of science are not the only way of arriving at knowledge of the world.

Knowing. What is it to know? What is it to make the world intelligible? What is it to truly understand it? Until now, the procedure of science has been to describe the natural world under laws, formulated in mathematical symbols, and to explain events according to theories about whether a thing is, what it is, its connection with other things, the reasons for the connection (Aristotle's Four Causes).

Modern science thus renders the world around us "intelligible" by analyzing it in terms of its material structures and functions, "reducing" these structures and functions to molecular structures and functions, describing these molecular structures and functions in terms of particles and forces.

Now we seek a cosmological story which may serve the function that the great myths have always served: empowerment, vision and meaning for human life. That means giving an account of the universe, making the universe intelligible such that we may locate our own being and purposes within it.

Modern science has aspects of the story, but now we are faced with the task of telling the cosmological story as a whole. So far we have indicated the limits of science for doing this, especially at the fundamental explanation of events in terms of forces acting between atoms and molecules.

And we have indicated that science is limited in this way because it always approaches the universe from the outside. Science is limited to the data of sense.

We have said enough, I think, to show that the universe has a "within," and that in ourselves—and so far, in ourselves alone—we have access to this "within" of matter. Now our question becomes: what is it to make something intelligible? comprehendible? understandable?

The roots of understand mean "to stand among." Certainly, the materialistic accounts of the universe let us "stand among" as one being among other beings, sharing their molecular makeup. But this is a "standing among" which does not satisfy the human heart.

So I return to "our father Parmenides," to the ancient pre-Socratic philosopher, who together with Pythagoras and Heraclitus provided the foundation for Greek thought. Parmenides said that whatever is, is intelligible. He learned this truth by making a symbolic journey (conducted by goddesses) to realms beyond the Earth. He stands at the dawn of thought, but has formulated, in a nutshell, the faith which underpins both the scientific and religious traditions: whatever is, is intelligible. Whatever is, we can stand among.

To comprehend: *com*—with, *prendre*—to take. The meaning of all the terms for knowing is *kinship:* being together, being with, being like.

So far I have suggested that the deep sense of alienation, fear and aloneness we feel at being on Earth, at being in the universe, is because we feel it to be basically (the fact of evolution notwithstanding) unlike. We are part of it, formed of it, but not yet "together" with it.

I suggest that we have this point of view because we have not approached the cosmos from its inner side. We see only the outer shell, the camouflage perhaps of something deeper, something more like us than machinery is, however sophisticated that machinery may be.

Perhaps the real basis of ethics is fellow-feeling, what the Carmelite Edith Stein called "empathy." We know the expression, "do not judge another until you have walked ten miles in his moccasins." And perhaps "understanding" means describing the universe in such a way that we have fellow-feeling for it. There is an ancient principle which says: like knows like.

Is the universe the sort of place with which we may identify our very most essential, heart-felt, human essence? Yes.

Scientific knowing, by theories, distances us from the phenomena being explained, at the same time giving us mastery of the natural world. It was minds filled with welters of theory which Heidegger called "forgetful of being," and unable to hear the speech of being.

There is an ancient philosophical tradition, fully manifested in Hegel, which holds that "knowing" is overcoming the subject–object distinction. As an eastern sage put it: You can only know the ocean by being the ocean. There must be, not the intermediary of theory, but some direct relationship with the object.

Can we know other beings in this way? That would be to know their inward life. Can we become one with Earth in this way? For now, having torn ourselves loose from nature, we are ready to reidentify with her at a "higher" level. A whole new mode of relationship may soon take place.

Western mystics such as St. Teresa of Avila and St. John of the Cross speak of a state of "union with God." They witness to the claim that all knowledge of God is experiential.

Knowing is "making intelligible." "Making intelligible" is establishing kinship, likeness. Knowing is overcoming the subject–object distinction.

If this be so, our scientific accounts are ultimately unintelligible. The ultimate explainers of science—forces—are utterly opaque to intellect, that is to say, most unlike us, most alien to us. Science has our alienation from nature built into its very "aseptic" language.

It is time for new terms. We seek a language of reconciliation, with terms which may enable us to come, once again, into viable relationship with the Earth we despise, the Earth we reject, and are continuing to reject.

We need a new understanding of what the Earth, and the universe, are, and of knowing. Can we really commune with, identify with the Earth, in knowing? Abraham knew Sarah, Sarah knew Abraham; knowing is something like that.

New Wineskins for New Wine

It is time to reinterpret the new story. The prevalent modern materialistic interpretation of the universe has been challenged in four ways: unexplained explainers in the underpinnings (the forces); human separability from the body; the fact that the human is the key to the inner side of matter, revealing matter to have a psychic-spiritual origin; the uncanny sense of physicists that the universe has been expecting us.

What sort of universe are we in? We have suggested that consciousness is first, and only secondarily gives rise to matter and form. Anthropomorphism has been frowned upon by scientists in the past in favor of a mechanical language of cause and effect. The value of "anthropomorphic," i.e., that we matter to the universe, has been summarized, and we have recounted the acceptance by many modern physicists of the anthropic principle.

Let us, then, be truly anthropomorphic. We must be so, because it is our account, given to establish our place in the scheme of things. Our account of the universe is given in language. In giving a description of the universe, everything depends, as in talking to a friend, on the terms we use. We can alienate ourselves from the other, or associate ourselves. It is all a function of a choice of words. And a choice must be made. Language is indeed mythical. Let us, then, be bold.

The sterility of the scientific account, as far as providing our needed cosmology goes, is a function of its language. Forces are, in fact, "occult entities," yet by means of them we are supposed to try to make the world intelligible. The word suggests we know something about the nature of the event through intuitive associations but, in fact, we know very little about the event. Science is truly mythical at this point. It is an inadequate myth. The machine must go. An undifferentiated field of energy is no help either. (Energy: "the ability to do work." What does the work? No one knows.)

Let us recall, at this point, something most scientists have forgotten. Newton, who originated the whole terminology of mechanism, believed that every body, far from being a billiard ball, had within it an "animating principle," which was the true source of what was revealed outwardly as "force." We have kept the forces and dropped this "life of bodies" just as we kept Pythagoras' mathematical ratios of tones and dropped the harmony of the sphere, just as we have valued the masculine at the expense of the feminine. All this may be a form of patriarchal predilection. It is time to recall Newton's insight. Modern materialism and mechanism are both forms of atomism, typical of the separated consciousness that the male is. Relationship with Earth requires a new understanding, the appropriate terminology of the unseparated form of consciousness, the sense of unity and wholeness, that is distinctly feminine.

In what terms, then, shall we give a fuller account? Tom Berry, geologian, and Brian Swimme, physicist, were talking together one night in a New York restaurant, and Tom said to Brian: "You physicists have the most stupendous account of the universe ever given, but the spiritual traditions have all the sweetness."

The spiritual traditions call the entity who stands at the beginning of all things, God. For most, this term is too full of bad connotations to be useful any longer, so we must endeavor to speak of this reality in other ways.

It is the power which created, originated and supports all derivative realities. It is intelligence. It confers order and meaning on what we do and are, and on the universe. It is the sense of being present to one another that we call "love." It is creative. In a word, all the attributes of consciousness—God is infinite consciousness.

Let us speak of this reality which stands at the "beginning" of all things and underpins the process, as Spirit, and by Spirit understand all of the above. The term "God" will be used only when it is necessary to tie into the religious traditions.

Heeding Tom's words, Brian Swimme wrote a book called *The Universe Is a Green Dragon*, in which he rewrites the fundamental vocabulary of physics to show just how magical the universe really is.

The approach taken here will be different. Comparisons have been made between the great advances of science since the Middle Ages, and the relative emptiness and sterility of theology. Let us try to rectify this imbalance. Let us begin with the spiritual traditions, returning to the scientific traditions through their mediation.

What is the justification for doing this? First, the religious account is not, as many scientists think, a more primitive account than the scientific. It is older, it is more fundamental. It is the earlier and more general self-revelation of the universe. The scientific account flows out of it, elaborates and validates deeper religious insights. The scientific belief in the orderliness of nature owes much to religious faith.

Second, the essence of the religious account is that intelligence formed the universe, that everywhere there is an element of design. Even modern physicists are beginning to subscribe to this modest claim. It has been suggested that the physicists climbing up the mountain are suddenly coming upon the theologians, having tea and saying: we thought you boys would never get here. The time is ripe for the synthesis of traditions which have been divergent, for good reasons, for a long time.

The religious tradition has often been terribly distorted through the ages, and abused for human purposes, but its essence is that the world developed out of Spirit. Spirit is unseen, invisible, primary and eternal. The whole of creation formed out of Spirit. Spirit is first and the visible is, in a deep sense, second. Creation is hospitable to the human, and Spirit cares for us. Those are the most essential elements of the spiritual account.

All the "splits and separations" of patriarchy, many of the categories of philosophy, the dualisms of the Piscean Age, and patriarchal models for knowing, derive ultimately from our stories, from the ways in which we have told our creation story. God is outside creation, as man is outside nature and woman.

We have considered the new story and many of its implications, and then taken the arduous path of argument in order to ascertain whether that story, as it stands, is sufficient for us. Now let us refresh ourselves with another story. Let us engage in a story of creation which may be instructive for us, told from its inner side, in that aspect of Spirit which we most need to hear. We are ready for such a story. The universe does not want this exquisite blue-green jewel of a planet, Earth, to disappear from the scene.

A Story of Beginnings

In the beginning was love, and love dwelt alone.

Love dreamed and brooded in itself, in its own vast imagination.

There love dreamed of all the offspring of love.

Love dreamed space and time, and the darkness of night. Love dreamed the many stars to light up the darkness, and planets about the stars. And love dreamed for each planet, its own particular life and being and character.

Love dreamed, and imagined, and thought.

Love dreamed of beings, innumerable beings, beings of all degrees and kinds, shapes and forms, in a spectacular array, with every conceivable consciousness, and lives of their own. Love dreamed of worlds visible, worlds invisible, of pure intelligence, of intelligence embodied.

And in its dreaming and imagining, love peopled the many planets in the vast recesses of space with these beings.

Among the planets love peopled in love's imagination, far off in a distant corner of its imagined universe, love saw a beautiful blue-green planet love called Earth. To Earth love gave mountains and hills, the great oceans, fish to swim in the seas, plants and animals to fill the land, the swift birds of the air.

Love brooded and dreamed Earth.

And love dreamed of another kind of being, one who would not be content to let plants and animals, or sunset and dawn, or the stars, or its own fragmentary life and times, pass unnoticed and unknown, one who would open itself to all existence and time and eternity, and record them in form invisible yet imperishable, a being in love with its own origins, a being in love with the eternal.

And so love dreamed, and imagined, and thought. Love dreamed the human, and gave it the word—images and ideas like love's own, the power and glory of forming invisible worlds, of giving the universe speech.

In the beginning was love, and love dwelt alone, wondering how to give these beings, these offspring, love's own, worlds beyond worlds and worlds within worlds, freedom and form. Love wondered how to make its very self real.

And so the first question was born.

In the depths of eternity, the answer came.

Love, seeing the way, could no longer contain itself, and burst into form.

And the universe began, in a blaze of light.

A New Universe

In the beginning was the dream. Now we can let our spirits soar.

I first encountered God while teaching Great Books at St. John's College in the desert of New Mexico. After I discovered the sciences could not explain the world, I took up the study of philosophy. Through those studies, I began to suspect his/her/its existence and reality. In a year of aridity and darkness, a student told me about a monastery over the hill I "must visit." It was the Benedictine and Charismatic monastery of Pecos, New Mexico. I went.

I took one look at the joyous faces of the mixed community of men and women there, and knew they had the truth. But what was it? I went back many times that Spring to find out, and later joined them for awhile to learn more of the mysteries. That joy, so different from what one finds in academic life, was the truth I sought. As well as stepping into the truth, I stepped into the living waters of the feminine, in a life of prayer, after studying all the patriarchal traditions of the west.

There, in a community of men and women where everyone sought to develop their feminine sides—it is our anima functions, our openness, our receptivity that can open up to God in prayer—I entered the rich, warm waters that the love of God is. I have been living with God ever since.

I learned there in the fires of the Holy Spirit that all knowledge of God is experiential, the doctrines and creeds of today have been elaborated out of some person's experience many centuries ago. Whereas for science the world is inert, simply "facts," in God, the whole world speaks. God is always addressing us, through the words of others, through the order of our lives.

It is as a messenger of the world that speaks, of God in creation, that I turn now to our first great concepts, the universe (a new universe) and Spirit (a new heaven). It was finally the omnipresent speech of God that taught me to listen to the Earth (a new Earth).

Love is a form of consciousness. It is that form of consciousness which accepts, which cares, which is non-judgmental. So a universe has come into being hospitable to every creature within it. Out of the ancient accounts, I retain the knowledge that God is love.

Now we must draw out of our premise—that the visible world of matter emerged out of the love-consciousness of Spirit—new conceptions of God, the universe, the Earth, and finally, ourselves.

Creation emerged by stages from a source in consciousness, and all the ultimate explanatory principles belong to consciousness. Not simply consciousness, but divine consciousness. The universe, as a whole, has goodness built into it, as Plato suspected. Science gives us the outer description of events; now, with the help of Brian Swimme, let us turn to the inner.

Let us image how the universe came to be from the inside. The universe grows like an organism or a human being, expanding and realizing the full range of its possibilities, and new possibilities, for consciousness is endlessly creative, and it is quite possible, if the universe came to be out of Spirit, that newness can enter the process at any time. The universe is not running down. Why did it emerge? For joy, plenitude, fullness of being.

The universe went from nothing to twenty-six trillion miles across in three seconds. What was the "stuff" of the explosion? Consciousness. The consciousness of love, which I call Spirit. The universe is Spirit incarnating into form.

The heat was immense. The exuberance of creation. The joy of it. No entity could withstand the temperature. And then, the cooling process began. The excitement as each entity came into being, discovering it was real, free, spiritual, endowed with so many properties of Spirit.

Scientists say opposite charges attracted, like charges repelled. That really means that electrons caught a glimpse of protons and were fascinated by them (Brian Swimme). In ecstasy they plunged into one another, forming the most stable union of any two beings, a polarity at the basis of the universe still reflected in our polarities.

The now stable nuclei discovered one another, and with a glad vibration, formed helium. As the mixture cooled, helium discovered more of its kind, and formed more complex elements, all with great excitement as if assembling for a pageant. If the rate had differed by one part per trillion, we would not be here. The universe would have been a chaos instead of a cosmos, an insane world. As it was—"contained exuberance."

The particles catapulted outwards into space. The wonder at their beings, at their incredible beauty and potential! What was it like to be the first "material" beings? Did they know glory in the divine darkness? Even atoms, with consciousness, might have sensed the adventure of it all. Could they feel what was possible to them? These atoms, the fundamental units of matter, have been the aim of our search since ancient times. It was with joy the elements discovered on another, and joy is the true foundation of the universe.

Billions of years went by of cooling, drifting, dreaming, expanding experience, realizing possibilities, discovering and building up those habits which we call "the properties of matter," which would rival those of Spirit. Elements aggregated, stable complexes formed, swirls, dust, rocks. Slowly, over billions of years—the universe is patient—stars, galaxies, planets, formed in care, that one day could be said the words: It is good.

Planets, our Earth and the rest of the solar system, were flung out about the sun some five billion years ago, an exciting, daring, creative event. God is a gambler and a dreamer (Tom Berry). Spirit quite likely does not order the behavior of atoms by "governing them according to laws," but by being an innermost part of their own nature, out of which they create their own realities. The universe is full of value and meaning.

The planets in our solar system ceased their explorations early. But Earth? Earth, with long, slow inventiveness, has been exploring her own possibilities. Her potential is so great. Temperature—just the right distance from the sun; size—just enough gravity to hold elements to the surface, but not too much to bind them so tightly they couldn't explore. Earth is a very special planet in the solar system.

The drama of Earth, the fateful, fruitful life of Earth, began in the ecstatic discovery of oxygen by hydrogen, forming a combination to produce the most mysterious of all beings, water, the most beautiful of the ancient elements, transparent, blue-grey to sky and cloud, lighted by the sun, endlessly lapping and tugging at rocky shores. The infinite possibilities of water.

Carbon, in this environment, explored its possibilities. Long, snake-like chains of carbon, just right for support systems, the basic structures for life, mirrored in our backbones. Together with oxygen, nitrogen, and hydrogen, carbon built up living systems.

The great variety of life is made possible by the distance apart of living beings. Just as the electrical forces attract and repel, so there is an attraction—an interest—of everything for everything else. But there is a balance in the whole, an interest strong enough to keep everything together, not so strong as to overcrowd.

Such are the primary entities which make up our beings. The atoms, far from being inert billiard balls bouncing off one another in the void, are creative centers of consciousness, full of light and love and daring.

Then life emerged in the early seas. The story of Earth's experimentation is well-known—single-cells, multicellular organisms, sponges, coelenterates, tunicates, worms, all the fantastical array of invertebrates, passing through backbones into the vertebrates, fish, amphibians, reptiles, birds, mammals, in intricate balance of prey-predator relationships, niches, zones, levels and depths. Their variety attests to the fantasy, the inventiveness, the creative play of it all, the imagination behind it, the grandeur and fun of the divinity in Earth.

Modern science locates all this in chromosomes. Animals are "pushed from behind." But chromosomes only express themselves in cells, surrounded by a whole organism. Perhaps, in fact, that just as with the big bang, consciousness was first, now consciousness precedes form. That is the cardinal principle of the universe; we realize it in everything we do, and it is the exact opposite of the prevailing assumption of modern science. In a universe which originated in consciousness, teleology is everywhere. How like ourselves the universe is! We are mirrors for one another. The doctrines of mechanism reflected the human poverty of spirit, as the emerging doctrines reflect its emergence into fullness of being.

How does it work? Perhaps this way. The species dreams a dream. This collective dream is of a new form, a form more diverse, more beautiful, more intelligent (or so it thinks) and the species as a whole makes a precognitive leap and programs its own genetic necessities. The genes are not "first" and the whole animal second, but genes are like money in the bank to be drawn out at will. But the physical world is deeply dependent on the spiritual world from whence it sprang, and is not self-sufficient as modern theories would have us believe. In the cooperation of dimensions, the consciousness of an animal comes first, and it assembles about it the material expression of that consciousness. This theory at present may seem farfetched; modern science will soon be confirming it.

So many forms of consciousness, so many different ways of experiencing the universe. The universe exults in its own being. And the whole spectacular array has emerged out of desire, out of curiosity and dream, out of that great joy which is the true foundation of the universe. And sexuality? The joy which the universe takes in its own being manifested in us, very deep in the nature of things, reflecting a polarity right from the beginning.

The impulse behind the whole? Desire. The desire of the Earth, which is embodied in each one of us, to realize all her potentialities. The visible universe is an achievement in form, but form is just the vehicle for consciousness, experience in the physical. Necessity is the "bread and wine" of metaphysicians. The true necessities in the universe do not originate in mechanism, but in desire, and desire is born of joy.

So we come to the human. Human beings come to the interbalanced whole, inventing language, learning manners, founding cities, distancing themselves from nature, not content to merely be a part but wanting to make all this explicit, in language. We wanted to know where we came from. We felt what may be a new emotion in the scheme of things: awe. We worshipped, and the centuries have refined our notions of what we worshipped. We arrived here two million years ago; we have been writing things down for a few thousand.

We are modes of Earth. What was Earth doing in its most recent, most dangerous experiment? Seeking to become aware of itself, to embody itself, as the poet Rilke put it, in invisible form—poetry, painting, music, literature, philosophy. And beyond Earth, the universe, seeking to experience itself in yet one more way.

In the fullness of time, Moses, Christ and Buddha came, to reveal the nature of the universe, and the appropriate human way of life within it. We unfold out of their stories.

In culture, we have realized the imagination of the Earth, a new and beautiful dimension of physical and conscious being. Now we are just leaving behind us the scientific-technological era.

What we are beginning to realize now, the legacy of Jerusalem, is that all knowledge comes through revelation. Earth has raised us up to peer at the stars, to reflect on ourselves, our natures and our origins. We invented science and explored creation with it, divesting it both of consciousness and magic. But the universe appears to be in search of the human. We are given no more than we are ready for. Only gradually is the curtain pulled back, are the veils lifted. We have to be ready. Perhaps we have to be worthy. The best secrets are still being kept.

The universe is like us, and we are like the universe. We belong here. We are not the lords of creation and it has not all simply been made for us. Neither are we without meaning or significance. We are beginning to realize we are important, we have some part to play, but we do not know just what it is. We belong to Earth, we belong to the cosmos. All beings are conscious, and consciousness knows no real boundaries.

Who are we among all the other animals? Teilhard de Chardin defined us simply as: "that being in which the universe reflects on itself." We still think of ourselves atomistically; we have not yet fully grasped the extent of our connectedness. But if all beings have consciousness . . . ! And here we rewrite Descartes' premises which alienated us from the rest of being. I say: Far from there being mind and matter, with the Earth and all her inhabitants being matter, matter and mind are everywhere together. The physical and the spiritual are always combined. So we have our new premise: No matter without mind. In the discussions to follow, we shall come to this again and again.

So, out of western traditions of thought, we have arrived at a metaphysics very similar to that of the North American native peoples. The universe is doing a new thing. We need a whole new understanding of God, that aspect of Spirit to which we can relate. For just as we are modes of Earth and modes of the universe, so these are modes of God. Modern culture is old, tired, a long way from magic and from its origins. As the philosopher Heidegger puts it, "The impulse to think was for the ancients, wonder; for Descartes, doubt; for the moderns, despair."

Courage—those are the phases of what the mystic St. John of the Cross described as a dark night of the soul. At the dark night's end is a new vision of God.

So now, we are ready to say something about what God is, a summary and extension, an inclusion and overcoming of the great tradition before us.

A New Heaven

Incarnation

Love is a mystery: Love *is* the mystery. We must begin with love. What have we said of love? That out of love, the fullness of Being comes, and such has deep implications for the Earth.

Love is the mystery. One of the many names of love is Spirit. We have said that God is an aspect of Spirit. At the very least, Spirit is here, and this will give us a whole new way both of understanding our lives and of looking at Earth.

First, Spirit comes first, and precedes all of creation, visible and invisible. Second, everything is Spirit. What else was there, in the beginning? Where has everything come from, if not from the very substance of God? Spirit overflowed out of itself with the necessity of a fountain spilling over, and out of its own inner being, formed every existing creature. Classically, Spirit was described as Spirit immanent and Spirit transcendent. The term "immanent" suggests there is something which is not God, but in which God dwells. This cannot be. There was only ever Spirit, and all things have emerged from Spirit's inner depths. This is to elaborate the term "God immanent," but since there is nothing but Spirit, the true distinction is between Spirit formless and Spirit formed. Hegel, the eighteenth-century metaphysician, realizing this truth, described creation as Spirit external to itself. The entire universe is the self-expression of God.

Spirit, infinite consciousness, is both beyond creation, and is the very substrate of creation. You must try to fathom this. What else could it be?

70

Third, we must say not that God made the world, but that God engendered creation. Spirit birthed the cosmos, visible and invisible, from its own being. Thus, all beings are the offspring of Spirit. Put another way, we may say that all are in the image of God. The animals and plants, the wolf, the tiger, the fly, the cactus, the entire planet, are as much made in the image of God as we are. This is the essential premise of creation spirituality. The sacred community consists not just of God and human beings, but all beings are included in it.

Fourth, from our human perspective, which often needs to "find" God, we may say: The whole cosmos is enspirited. That is to say, the universe is God's body, made by God. Spirit is everywhere, in all things, and God—the living God, the God of touch—will come to us from any part, from a swirl of snow, a tree, a pigeon's beady eye, the depths of our beings. God is always touching us. We miss these touches because our minds are full of false distinctions, and we do not expect them.

Fifth, the universe is one in Spirit. The insight of the Greeks was, "All is one." The revelation to the Hebrews, "I am one."

These are the five major implications of our new story for our understanding of God. They follow from our account. All have far-reaching implications for us, for the way we live, for how we treat the Earth. The most difficult to understand is the fifth. What does it mean to say the universe is one? In what way is it one?

All universes are born of consciousness. Matter, the physical world, is simply consciousness in a highly condensed form. God is consciousness rarefied, and human beings are somewhere in between. What in the past became a matter/spirit dualism is really a continuum and a matter of degree. And since the "stuff" of this continuum is consciousness, we can say that the entire universe is spiritual rather than "material," to employ an old distinction. This theory is the exact opposite of the theories of modern science. And all beings are in relationships of various kinds, for consciousness knows no absolute boundary.

So, we are ready to rewrite Descartes' premises in an even more ultimate way than, "no matter without mind." We can say, "all matter is mind." Now we are in a whole new era of thought, ready to free ourselves from the tyranny of mechanism and materialism which have dominated the past three hundred years.

We may need metaphors to talk about the universe. Perhaps the universe is like a painting by Matisse. Matisse worked with a sense of the whole. A first daub of color here would suggest another daub of color there, then a line, a certain form, etc. A certain idea of what was to be achieved, a "theme" guided the emergence of a finished painting which was a unity of many elements. The universe is the composite of painting and painter.

The universe is expanding, dynamic, emergent, developmental. This means as stars, galaxies, pull apart, they remain in association through attractive forces of gravity, but now new developments may take place as the interactions weaken. The universe develops as a game develops in which children, running, toss a ball back and forth among them.

Perhaps the universe is like a human life developing. A human life is a very rich and deep thing. There is a physical form, changing through life and through experience. But there is an inner being. A person develops for a long time, then discovers who it is, what it likes, what it prefers to think about, what it is in its community, its city, its country, its world, the planet, comes across words which seem to name it, modifies its behavior accordingly, guides itself by changing conceptions of itself. We need self-identity, the interplay of who and what we are with our words for ourselves. We need an ever-deepening sense of who this "I Am" is. (Perhaps that is why Spirit exploded into a universe.) We seem to be a peculiar mixture of "self-realizing" "self-making" and "self-discovery." And all our journeys, the people we meet, the books we read, the whole universe, are involved in the process.

Or perhaps Spirit develops as a written work. Everything to come is contained in the first sentence, but the whole does not emerge out of that sentence in any simple way. Yet, when it does come, it is exactly right. So the universe is being written as scripture is written, anticipating all possible readers, with this difference: there is no last line.

One of the best models for how the universe might unfold comes from the east. It is twenty questions, and one person is out. When she comes in, she asks the first member of the group whether it is animal, vegetable or mineral. The first person must have some definite concept in mind of some thing, which has not been told to the others, and answer accordingly. If he answers "animal," all the others must continue with this category, but with their own object. So the game goes, and so the universe differentiates as the consequence of first, and subsequent, choices.

And what is the human in this universe that is the self-expression of love? *A fragment of Spirit.* The infinite consciousness of God contained in a body.

How close God is! The God of our heart's desire dwells within us.

"Chance and Necessity" versus "Design"

If the universe emerged out of consciousness, then it is full of design, which Plato contrasted with "chance and necessity." At this point we live, for the most part, in a chance and necessity universe, and modern ideologies are Cartesian. We are material beings in a material universe; we live like any animal—we are born, grow old and die. Death is the end of things. We procreate, we work to earn our food. We try to further the well-being of our species. And while we are here, our art, literature, newspapers, entertain us.

What happens to that deep question about the meaning of life posed by every human heart? Some would say that it is a sentimental, irrelevant question which has no meaning. It is best left to artists and poets. Since they are "only artists," no one really cares what they say. The human race developed through material process by chance and necessity, is the dominant animal in its environment, and can employ the other animals as it wishes in the best interests of human well-being. Man is the measure of all things. We are the source of our own values, common sense is sufficient for the difficult questions, ideas of

God are "ideology" and sentimentality, the whole universe came to be by chance, and to ask if human life has purposes beyond perpetuating itself makes no sense.

This mechanistic atomism fuels corporate and multinational mentalities, and the minds of many of those who make our decisions. It has been called "the mechanistic paradigm." Let's make the most of things while we're here, produce, make money, enjoy comfort, business as usual, the growth economy and so on. The world, in such a view, would look better paved.

Our technological society, with its ethic of, "if it can be done, do it," is underpinned by metaphysical assumptions about matter and the ultimacy of the scientific account which are false. They belong to an old legacy which is passing away. But only if we can lay bare the truth of the universe shall we have a touchstone against which to judge the technological prescriptions for human life and the "management" of the Earth.

What would it mean for us to live in a universe of design? First, that we are willed here, that we are wanted here, that we are here for a reason.

Second, the universe contains all that our hearts intuited was there—intelligence, wisdom, care, love, are not just in us but are deep in the nature of things.

Third, intelligence is at work, in the universe as well as in us. The source of the universe is infinite consciousness, so we can say the universe is a story which has an author, even if that author is within the story. We pack our little human stories with foreshadowing, symbols, characters, plot and meaning . . . missing from the scientific account, which gives us only facts . . . and missing from our lives. If we can do so much with our little human stories, how much more must the author of the universe (from which our little stories are all derivative) have packed into the larger story of itself? We have not yet begun to decipher the meanings of the larger story for ourselves, let alone for what it reveals about its author. History—natural and human—is the biography of God (Tom Berry).

Fourth, if there is design in the universe as a whole, there is design in human life. We have thought of ourselves as "atoms in the void," trying to take responsibility for things, "masters and mistresses of our own fates," going about our business tense, nervous, for the most part deeply alienated from the natural order. But what if perhaps there is a plan?

If the universe has a designer who works in and through the universe in its emerging stages, the full meaning for us is that someone else is running the show, therefore, relax.

It has been said: "The very hairs of your head are numbered." With design in the universe as a whole, what about our human lives? Could it be that we are being held, from first to last, in a deep care? Could it be that just when we think we are all alone, we are surrounded by a cocoon of love? Could it be that when we are planning a day, it is "being planned?" Perhaps the people in our lives are neither "responsibilities" nor "commitments," words fashionable nowadays, but are gifts and messengers, and we are meant to develop in some way not understood by modern culture? Spirit may have a will for us, mysteriously bound up in our own free choices; we can go with the grain of reality or against it. Spirit may speak its words to us through the speech of others. Spirit's words may be rustling all about us, but we do not hear them because we do not expect them; the day may be, from first to last, a message of guidance and care; the city, the universe, may "speak" to us (in the scientific account, it is inert). We have thought we were the author of our lives, but perhaps we are only co-author, a truth which will annoy some, and comfort many. Indeed, perhaps our lives are not just a story, but a mystery. In short, our little life here is laced by the greater life of God.

For Spirit is here, with its guidance, its care of us, the divine energies in the matrix of existence. We have to learn to see. Go forth, not to do business or observe the human, but to meet God, and you will find God everywhere.

Perhaps we are here for a reason, and life and Earth are schools for us. There may be a plan for us, a plan for Earth. And if there are plans—something which has been denied throughout all the mechanistic era—shouldn't we want to know what they are? One can be a good pupil or a slow one, an attentive listener or one distracted by the many false doctrines of the day that are being lived out everywhere.

If Spirit is real, part of the process, then all our heartfelt questions about meaning and purpose, dismissed as irrelevant by modern science, have a place. And we can ask: does God have a plan for my life? Clearly, if there is an overall theme, an implicit design for the universe, we can frustrate it or further it. So, there may be what can only be called spiritual principles of life, principles which harmonize spirit and Spirit, and teach us how to live. The greatest of these principles is that consciousness must create, that we create our realities from our consciousness, and those created with love have the greatest effect.

How should we live is the fundamental human question. Today this question is being answered by scientists, psychologists, technocrats and governments. We need to know the truth about the universe to answer this question properly for ourselves, and in order to limit our technology. The most important aspect of that question concerns our relationship to Spirit. How should a fragment of Spirit live?

God the Beloved

Who are we, in the context of Spirit? The revelation of Spirit to Moses is usually translated as: I am. I am who am. An alternative translation reads: I am who I will be. Yes, the developing universe.

Jesus, in the New Testament, revealed Spirit as close to each one of us, as wholly loving, forgiving, merciful. Jesus experienced for himself this closeness of Spirit, called it "Father," and taught a way of life to bring us to this closeness. Spirit is something we can have a personal relationship to, and is to be found in our own depths.

Christianity has been preoccupied with the personality of Jesus (often forgetting his message of our own empowerment) because Jesus was called Son of God, and said of himself: Whoever has seen me has seen the Father. Since we were told that we are made in the image of God, we want to know what God is like that we may know how to be.

What do we see in Jesus? He spoke with authority. He was at ease in the cosmos, at home everywhere, always out-of-doors.

He could talk to anyone and he cared especially for the wretched of the Earth. He was vehement against the abuse of knowledge, and the corruption of children. He taught and healed. He was often at prayer. He seems to have been a deeply whole man in the Jungian sense. But most of all, he knew exactly who he was for the Father.

The revelation of Jesus was that as Spirit cares deeply for each one of us, so we should care for ourselves, and for each other, and that the first commandment is simply to love God. What is God like, that we may love?

Spirit is revealing itself to physicists at the frontiers of science as a lover of surprises. To those who realize that creation embodies Spirit, Spirit reveals itself as a profound, deep, intriguing, exciting dimension of reality, like a beautiful woman dwelling in mystery, revealing glimpses of herself in unexpected moments, as a lover. Spirit delights in revealing itself to us, but not until we are ready.

For the tradition of the past age, we have been "children of God." It is wonderful to curl up in an accepting, parental love. But this term sets us apart from all other beings on the planet, and finally from God, of whom we can be afraid. For parents are "above" children, they have secrets from children, sometimes they punish. And they always repress sexuality.

We are growing up. The Father image was fine when we were little children, but is now inadequate for what the universe is revealing Spirit to be—a fathomless, accepting love embodied in the whole of creation. We are children of the planet and must go to school with it. For Spirit, we are rapidly becoming something else. The past ages were a time of formation. Now we are ready to soar on a new understanding of human identity.

A daughter knows the Father is really the beloved. Spirit, formerly called Father, can now be called: beloved. A beloved is not "above" us, does not keep secrets from us as parents do, and does not punish. He is beside us, expounding to us all of his sacred mysteries, which he wishes us to share, circling us round, taking us by the hand, leading us, guiding us—by touch, by words—challenging us, provoking us, full of love, laughter, tenderness, and the many surprises which only a beloved can give. In our age, women know what Spirit is like. In the future, children will reveal it. Later, as we learn their languages, the animals, the leaves, and blades of grass will reveal the nature of the Source.

Spirit cannot be imaged. Spirit is within the process as well as beyond it, and signifies the kind of relationship which we may take up with it. Spirit cannot be thought about or described (it is well to remember this in an age top-heavy with doctrine). But Spirit can be known—and this is God's revelation to women—God can be known through inner touch, through experience. Such knowledge will come to us from any part of creation.

So, you find God when you least expect God—when washing the dishes, doing the ironing, or getting on a bus. Spirit is our beloved. We are fragments of Spirit. We are beloved of the source of the universe. If we wish to delight an earthly beloved, how much more the Spirit of the universe. The question, "How should we live?" is really the questions, "What is God like, that we may imitate?" "What is it to be a true fragment of Spirit?"

We are ready for a greatly expanded spiritual path. All spiritual paths begin in the knowledge that one is deeply loved by Spirit. Such knowledge gives us courage for everything else, and that is the truth on which our lives must be founded.

The ideal of former times was the ideal of the saint, the one who loved. To be like God was to love, and so we imitated the saints.

Today, our ideal is different. Our ideal is the genius, the creative person. Everyone is some kind of genius in his/her own life. Previous ideals are not abolished; the way of truly loving those around us is an ongoing discovery, but the human self is ready to burst its fetters. We are giants, living like pygmies, perpetually caught in "the glance of the other" (Sartre). The universe is courting a new mode of human being. A creative being. For the beloved is Spirit-creator.

The new spiritual path is the creative path. This requires a new understanding of the self, for one is going to "hassle" oneself. Are we the strange animal, to have such a path? No, the animals have already found theirs, in what we call "instinct."

We come to identity and true self-knowledge, like God, through our works.

We all yearn for knowledge of Spirit. What does our story of the universe reveal about the originator of the story? We have knowledge by inference from the story, and we have direct knowing, by communion, in which the subject/object distinction is overcome.

Let us consider what creation reveals of the creator, our indirect knowledge. Finally, we shall speak of direct experiential knowing.

Creation and Creator

What can we say of the creative Spirit of the universe? Let us try to see as God sees, the magic of our planet. Let us look with a fresh glance upon the things around us.

The creator is immensely patient. Twenty billion years, to get to us. The creator is careful—every part had to be fitted to every other part, the timing just right for what, on Earth, has been a dangerous experiment.

What can we say of the creator as we observe all around us the results of its rich imagination? What can we say of the creator's loves and dreams?

The creator loved color. God could have made a black-and-white universe. Color is a great miracle: everywhere we look there is color, in every shade and hue imaginable—the reds and mauves, purples and golds of dawn and sunset, the dark strange blues and greys of clouds before a storm, the greens of grasses, plants and trees, the changing blues, greens and greys of the sea, the pale browns and beiges of the bare countryside on a winter's day, the black of tree trunks, not to mention the delicate hues of the forest and the colors of birds and flowers.

The creator loved shapes—bare branches, animal shapes, delicately pointed leaves.

The creator loved texture—fuzzy bees, slippery smooth fish, prickly nuts and porcupines, the different barks of trees.

And the creator loved sounds. We could be living in a soundless world, but instead we have the early morning chorus of birds, the sound of wind in the trees, of rain on the roof, of waves on the shore, of the clinking of ice breaking up on a Spring night. Sound—a cat's meow, a dog's bark, the eerie call of the loon, frogs in chorus in the Spring evening. The cosmos is full of sound, and voice, and a music which fills space, which Pythagoras at the dawn of written history called "the Music of the Spheres."

The creator loved variety. God was not satisfied with one kind of fish but so many different kinds of fish. And so it is for all the other animals, for ducks and frogs, for penguins and earthworms, and thousands of kinds of insects. The creator has not simply favored the human—one instrument—but wanted a full orchestra.

The creator works with little waste of material. Nothing is lost in nature, or superfluous, but everything is recycled. Nature is an organic whole, which does not increase entropy. The creator builds one element after another, one flora after another, one fauna after another—all is a meaningful crescendo.

The creator harmonizes—the growth of trees in the appropriate season, the reproduction of animals when the offspring can best survive, the wonderful adaptations of animals to their environments.

The providential care that has been taken with each being— each has its place in the economy of the whole, each has its source of good, its proper knowledge of how to live. The animals and birds are ever busy raising their young, but they are not anxious and do not waste.

And Beauty! The creator had an eye to what we could experience as beauty—the beauty of the changing seasons, taskteachers that they often are, the soft grey rains of Spring, the dazzling winter light and snow, autumn colors, summer storms—the beauty of our lives, and in our lives, is immeasurable. We have only forgotten that we are part of the whole.

What sort of a creator is it who decided that the most important lessons of life should be learned at play, while we were growing up? And who decided that to exercise our bodies should fill us with elation? Who decreed that we should feel, that we should thrill to the night sky, that we should feel awe, love, reverence, sorrow, which is what it is to be alive? He could indeed have made us little mechanisms, just merely reacting to events. Instead, there is all this inner life, and our imaginations, and the soul's depth of response, to poetry, music and art. This inner life is reflected in the infinite variety of human faces, and in that seriousness which is in everyone.

And who but a God of delight should have given us so much capacity for feeling in our bodies and souls, a yearning to be like God and to know God and to celebrate? God has given us the senses. To live in the universe in the senses is perhaps our most truly spiritual state.

And God has given us our sexuality—given it to all creatures—given us the deep experience of making love, in which we come to know him, in which we have a taste for what it was for love to explode into light, in the leap and dance of everything within us.

The beauty of the cosmos. The beauties of our life. God is good. We have only lost touch with God's world, the living, breathing, rhythmic cosmos. We have substituted for this world (which we have come to fear) a fabricated world of human invention, full of complex doctrines of God and human beings, and lots of "keep off the grass" signs. We have lost touch with our own true beings, and substituted for our intuitive knowledge of how to be a false world of authority, coercion, management "keeping us all in line." We must return to our place in the cosmos where we belong. Only in that context will we know what it is to be a fragment of Spirit. Only in that most ultimate context will we know how to live, and the true depths of the human being.

We are fragments of Spirit living on a most beautiful and magical planet, in an experience shot through with cosmic values.

Touching God

Spirit is here. We are fragments of Spirit. Spirit is love, and love we can experience. Spirit should be the most experienceable reality for us.

To be a fragment of Spirit is to have the most positive self-image of all. We are not an "image" of truth and reality, but *are* this truth and reality (although the authorities have always kept this from us). We are full of Spirit's mind, wisdom, power, love. All knowledge for this, and any, life, is within us, waiting to be tapped. Now, we take our shape, our way of life, from the stifling conventions of a fabricated civilization. But we know how to live; our deep source is within us. Our fabricated world would have us live mechanically, within endlessly structured lives, being "polite." Is this how the dynamic Spirit of the universe wants us to live?

How does a fragment of Spirit live? Fully, with every faculty alive, all modes and depths and heights, held together and integrated by love. That is what it is to be alive, to feel in oneself the deep substratum of joy in the universe, celebration, awareness of the mysteries, from deep within ourselves. Sometimes we are love exploding in the big bang, sometimes we are a restless river running to the sea, sometimes we are a still lake at evening. All the Earth is in us. And let us remember that as we are fragments of Spirit, so too is everything else—every duck, platypus, nasturtium and spider. A truly raised consciousness will attune to them, to know what kind of fragment of Spirit they are. A truly raised consciousness directs itself to Spirit, for Spirit is there, under a thousand forms. Our new story gives us the basis of a new spirituality.

To be the beloved of God implies a new way of worshipping. God is so close. Charismatic Christians discover that when they truly open themselves to praise, God comes in. We need to discover ways of worship which shall honor the Earth, and connect with the Spirit that is within Earth. We need to rejoin creation. We have no need for authorities, no one is "over us," God is in personal relationship to each one of us. When we gather to worship—let it be out of doors—we gather as equals. Let our worship be a total rejoining of our full beings with our source in a deep attunement to the universe and to all that is beyond the universe.

"Enspirited" is the term which describes the world in which

we find ourselves. Spirit will come to us from any tree or animal, for God dwells in the depths of each. Spirit cannot be imaged, but only touched with the inner senses. Spirit comes to us through our whole affective life of feeling and emotions. Love, light, life, power, peace, beauty, joy are the signs. Feel any of these, you have been touched by Spirit. Spirit comes to awaken us out of our cold, mechanical world, our Cartesian ways of being, so fully realized in modern civilization.

Spirit dwells in our depths, and will come to us through prayer and meditation. According to St. Teresa of Avila, prayer consists not in saying much, but in loving much. Yes, because God can only be experienced. Prayer has been variously defined: a lifting of the heart and mind to God; seeing as God sees; communion with God. There is a place for words in prayer, but they are special words. Words of the heart. One confides to God one's joys and sorrows, one's pain and fear and anxiety, and they are lifted. To the source of one's being, anything can be said.

For those who find prayer difficult, Earth is the way. One can dwell deep in one's body and soul, below the level of words. St. John of the Cross called silence "the Voice of God." We have a surface and a depth, and can dwell at different levels of reality and relationship. God is in the depths.

So, let us commune with the planet. Take up relationship with a tree. Attune yourself to a tree, and feel the love flow between you, because trees, despite all we have done to them, are fond of us. Put your hand to it and it will give you words and images for its being; the native shamans spoke to trees, and trees to them. Then go deeper, and fill yourself with the great energies of God, which are beyond mind and speech. Trees, too, are fragments of God.

These things can be verified by anyone. The true God, the God of magic for a mechanistic society, is just a few right ideas and the touch of a hand away. Knowing, until now, has preserved the subject–object distinction. True knowing is a union, an identity between knower and known. If all is matter, such knowing is not possible; if all is Spirit, such knowing is possible.

Spirit dwells in all creation. You are looking at a flower, and in a little inner swirl you are gazing into Spirit; a true smile penetrates your heart, and you are looking into the depths of eternity; a word overheard on a street corner lays all your problems to rest; you are getting on a bus, and inspiration wells up from the depths; a night of anxiety, and suddenly the room is filled with a redemptive presence. God is so close. If we go forth in the expectation of being touched by love in our inner beings, then love will come to us in a thousand forms. All the touches of God change the mind, and reveal, inwardly, the nature of Spirit. The physical dimension of existence is a light veil over the deeper reality of Spirit, consciousness is open-ended, and the consciousness of all beings ultimately merges with the deeper consciousness of Spirit. The separate state can be overcome through attunement, through touch.

The Spirit, who loves surprises, has awaited an uptight generation, a generation afraid of touch, afraid of expressing praise in its bodies and souls, afraid of laying hands on one another, afraid of being thought ridiculous by hugging a tree, to reveal how close, how accessible, it really is.

Spirit comes to us below the level of speech. Spirit is knowable, the most supremely knowable reality in the universe. But it is not known through theory, through "talk about." Words are extremely limited. It is known through experience. There is nothing each of us hungers for more than this. For God, if it be the whole of reality—and it cannot be anything less—is, for us, so often hidden. Most religions make God only a part of reality, the good things, the nice things, but God is everything. Yes, love, but also fear, joy, fatigue, embarrassment. All is a part of God, and God is part of everything, our science, music, poetry, art, our loves, our lives. God is not judgmental, but judgment is part of God. God embraces the totality, and our prayer ways are designed to get us closer to the essence. So, new age thinkers call God All That Is.

Now we know what the universe is—all causality is through consciousness. Now we know that Spirit is the whole of creation. All the news is good; how close God is, how touchable. These are the intellectual premises of mystical experience. We are ready for the turn to the Earth. What new ideas must we have about the Earth? What is the news of Earth? It means that in our new universe all comes to be from consciousness. Our new heaven means that God is in creation. Now we must consider the Earth.

A New Earth

The glory of the human is the
  desolation of the Earth.
The desolation of the Earth is the
  destiny of the human
All plans, policies, laws, institutions,
  ways of life, must be judged for
  their effects on the well-being
  of the Earth, do they harm, are they
  indifferent to, do they advance that
  well-being?

(Tom Berry, paraphrase)

We have spoken of a new heaven and a new universe. What does our new account of beginnings imply for the Earth?

On the premises that Earth is matter, a machine, and we are to "have dominion over her" we have almost done the planet in. Now we know that the correct reading of Genesis is "be responsible for," and that Earth is not a machine. It is time to sketch the outlines of a new Earth.

Positions which are true can be arrived at in a variety of ways. What I am going to say derives from our creation story, but it is also a fact of my wilderness experience.

For the better part of the past fourteen years I have lived a wilderness life in the hills of Cape Breton, Nova Scotia. My home is a two-story log house which I have shared with Don and Puss, with no indoor plumbing, no electricity and no telephone, along a forest track, one mile from the nearest plowed road. (If you want paradise, get rid of the telephone.) We get five feet of snow in the winter, a short summer growing season. Our outhouse commands a marvelous view of the valley below, and I would not trade it for any modern convenience. Deer and moose visit, we see the tracks of bear and coyotes, and hear the songs of coyotes and owls in the night.

I took up this life at the age of forty-one, after many years of studying science, philosophy and the spiritual traditions. I wanted a simple life of practical tasks, writing and prayer, to live completely with God. After the abstractions of academic life I have come to love words which are close to the Earth—wood, stone, cup, spruce.

That life has given me God. Its thousands of practical tasks grounded me, enabled me to assimilate all I had taken in during the first part of life, and brought me back into the cosmos of my childhood in a hands-on experiential way. I have come to love all its practical tasks, its silence, the winds, the winter storms, the depths of experience with the Earth it has made possible. I have explored being in simple ways, explored what a life can be, learned the joy of living in my body and senses. Snowshoeing in that first winter with fear in our hearts and the owls swooping and calling before us was magic.

Most deeply, I have learned that God can be experienced in the Earth, at a level far below the level of mind, coming to us through our feelings, our senses, our bodies, our deep psyches, and that the Earth allows deep mystical experience of God. All make it from time to time, but our Cartesian selves deny it.

I chose this life for God; God gave me the Earth. In living so close to the Earth, by some reading, by much experience and assimilation, I have come to know many truths about the Earth which I will summarize in four concepts.

The Earth is:
    living
    conscious
    spiritual
    divine.

These are powerful new conceptual lenses through which to approach the reality of the Earth. We have only been missing the radiance these past few centuries because our minds and souls are clogged with false ideas.

Earth Is a Living Being

The whole Earth is one living being. This notion was conceived by James Lovelock on a camping trip (*The Gaia Hypothesis*). He later proposed it to the scientific community, and this view is now endorsed by many scientists, and increasingly verified.

This is an idea of tremendous power, for it enables us to appropriate all the rich ways of thinking we have for organisms, for thinking about the Earth. Living organisms self-regulate, self-develop, self-heal. They maintain their state relatively constant, and the Earth has been doing these things for millions of years with no help from us. Organisms maintain homeostasis. They buffer themselves at relatively constant temperature and salinity. Organisms have limits of tolerance beyond which they cannot sustain themselves. Organisms have conditions which must be met if they are to flourish.

And most important, organisms are one; every part interacts with and is dependent on every other part, and damage to one part is passed along to all. Thus, pollution in the atmosphere circles the globe in eleven days; radioactive fallout in Russia turns up in the rain over Ottawa; cutting trees in India floods Bangladesh; cutting the rain forest in the Amazon affects climate everywhere; pesticides and herbicides used in agriculture to increase yields end up in the ground water, the drinking water, our foods, us; poisons pumped into the oceans are concentrated by microorganisms, picked up by birds and fish, concentrated thousands of times and returned to us in what we eat. If we persist in present practices, the human will be the first to go, done in by its own hand, because it is at the top of all the food chains.

This is a whole new way for us to think about the kind of reality Earth is. Far from being a linear array of mechanisms,

Earth consists of finely-tuned ecosystems, webs and cycles of interdependent, interconnected life forms, and those webs are fragile. The well-being of our lives depends on the well-being of every life on the planet. Organic notions are being forced upon us. We have to understand whole systems of living beings.

To say Earth is a living organism is a radical new way to think about the Earth after these past three hundred years of considering her to be mere matter. Knowing Earth is a living being will guide us in taking up the right relationship with her. At the very least, living beings have limits, and to respect those limits, to bring our civilization into balance with the living Earth, human beings are going to have to self-limit.

And this is because of one profound implication: In living beings, every part serves the whole, and every natural "resource" plays some part in the support and maintenance of the one organism the Earth is, not just ourselves. We have to get over thinking of the Earth as made specifically for us, as our property. We are a part of the Earth, and the Earth has her own reasons for being. We need to ask, before we cut, shoot or net anything: "What part does it play in the whole?"

Earth Is a Conscious, Spiritual Being

That Earth is a living being may teach us much about how to interact with her, but it may not yet bring us back to magic. So let us consider the next two powerful ideas for understanding the Earth. Earth is a conscious, spiritual being—intelligent, sentient, self-aware, having her own identity, of which we are a part. Earth is rightly called "she."

Our notion of Earth as a machine came from Descartes and has been our hidden premise all these centuries. The crisis in Earth calls this notion into question. "Those we look down upon are sent to renew us" and the bearers of culture are most often the outcast peoples (Tom Berry). The indigenous people are right. The ancient North American native peoples knew that every being is conscious and spiritual, and communicated freely with all. Imagine, if we could communicate with every form on the planet! This possibility is something each of us has to test out for themselves. The human is not alone here, imposing its will on an indifferent object. Nature, the Earth, is a subject, with her own deep interior life, full of subjects, and we can be in dialogue with them. We have lost our abilities to speak to the Earth, but some of the native peoples and a few others know how to communicate, and we can learn from them.

That is to say, Earth is more like us than we have ever suspected before; she has her own inner life as every being on the planet has its own inner life.

Before conscious, spiritual beings, reverence and respect are the appropriate attitudes. Human arrogance is appalling. We never ask the trees if we may cut them down, or which would be the best trees to take, as the native peoples did. We do not even say "thank-you," a minimal condition in any spiritual relationship. No being on Earth has any right to its own life except the human, and then only some human beings at the expense of others. The most important change which has to come about in us is a change in attitude. We have to learn respect, and then take what we need (not what we desire) from the place of respect. With such an attitude, technologies which pollute would never even be invented.

With living, conscious beings, one can communicate spirit to spirit via the inner senses. Put your hand to a tree, and ask it about itself or the Earth, about how you can help, and it will answer you in images or words floating up from your own depths. That is how animals, too, communicate with us, in images passed from soul to soul, much deeper, vivid and more accurate than any amount of human vocabulary taught to monkeys. When I am in Toronto, lying on my couch, my cat of nineteen years lies on my stomach and we commune together about all that we most love about Cape Breton, and she shows me her world as she sees it—grass blades, wet wooden steps, the hidden tunnels through raspberry canes. The animals still know the beauty of the planet. Try experiencing the woods as a deer experiences it, or the pond with the frogs of a spring night. Yes, there is magic. All the beings of the Earth are waiting to introduce us to a major enrichment of our own consciousness if we will open to theirs. These are things to be tried. They are possible because consciousness comes first, in the Earth, in every mosquito, snake, zebra and morning glory on the Earth, and form comes second.

So, again, on new grounds, the grounds of experience, we go beyond Descartes. The heart of all darkness is the premise that matter has no mind. We replace this with the pearl of great price: no matter without mind. The Earth and every being on her are animate, and we can be in an I–Thou relationship with all. We are ready to take up relationship to other beings, not by dissection, analysis or exploitation, but through conscious communication. It is time we all became friends with our first cousins here, the plants and animals.

Earth Is a Divine Being

Now let us take a step further. Not only is the Earth a living and conscious being, she is a divine being. God is in the Earth, indeed, the Earth is God under the accidents of shape, texture and color. Earth is now widely called Gaia. Gaia was the Greek goddess of the Earth, and it is well to remember that the shrine at Delphi was Gaia's long before it was Apollo's. Even scientists are using a name which speaks of the divinity of the Earth, a divinity they have never made explicit.

In 450 BC, Praxilla, a Greek woman poet wrote:

Most beautiful of things I leave is sunlight;
then come glazing stars and the moon's face;
then ripe cucumbers and apples and pears.

A male commentator of the time, Zenobios, said of Praxilla:

Only a simpleton would put cucumbers and the like
on a par with the sun and moon.

But Praxilla was right, and many women have always known that the Earth is a divine being. Now we can make explicit that this is so according to the tradition of thinking that says God is immanent in Earth. But it follows from our creation story, from the deep truth which all must finally come to recognize that there is only God, there is nothing but divinity. This is to greatly expand our notions of where God may be found. God is not up there, the Earth down here, God is in the Earth. Indeed, Earth is a form of Spirit, an embodiment of God in the physical plane of existence, a projection of God into the physical, if you will.

This is not to say that God is only in the Earth; God's reality goes far beyond the Earth, but one of God's forms is the physical universe, including the Earth. Another way of saying this is that the Earth has emerged from the depths of the spiritual world, which is part of God. This does not mean that we worship the Earth, any more than we worship the consecrated host, but we worship with and through the Earth the God who is in all.

The Earth is an expression of God. These are hard notions to grasp, but at the very least, they tell us that we can always find God in the Earth. Again, this is something the native North Americans have always known. Civilization is filled with the things we have made; nature is, as used to be said, the things God made, or as we now say, a form of Spirit. Nature exists at all levels and depths. Our senses make for us a lovely camouflage, but just beneath the surface are the great energies of God, and they will come to us through the senses. Walk through a wood, pause in the living silence, open yourself, and you will experience the divine presence. Before, among, and within divine beings, reverence, awe, a respectful tread and a listening, attentive ear and eye, are the appropriate responses. Let us go forth to live the truth of our own divinity in the divinity of the Earth that is all around us.

To say the entire Earth, the physical universe, is a form of God, is formed from God's consciousness, still allows for a distinction to be made between the rarefied, pure essence of God, and what is sometimes called Godhead, the condensed energies of God which appear as matter. The beauty of the continuum is that the pure essence of God is always flashing out to us from under its physical camouflage.

And so we have rewritten Cartesian premises entirely,

approximating to a new unity consciousness of Being after the dualisms of the Piscean age: all matter is mind.

An Earth-Centered Perspective

Our first paradigm shift was that consciousness comes first. We come now to our second paradigm shift, another "Copernican shift" from the human-centered perspective to an Earth-centered perspective. Back to the ancient beginnings, in a new way. Enough has been said to show that Earth is biologically prior to us and primary in the scheme of things, we are secondary; now we are coming to realize that she has all the very attributes of life, consciousness, spirituality and divinity which we are fond of attributing to ourselves. Animals and plants have a very different consciousness from us, but it is consciousness nevertheless, and all forms of consciousness are intrinsically without boundary.

An Earth-centered perspective means that Earth is the standard of all human activities, and this change in priorities is crucial if we are to bring human civilization into balance with the limits of a living Earth. Only cancer cells have unlimited "growth"; every other being lives within limits and since the human has outstripped its natural limits, it now has to voluntarily *self-limit*, the essence of all ethics. It can be helped in this if it refers its concerns to Earth, not to yet other human concerns. Earth is the standard from beyond the human on the human. Earth is not an idea but a reality beyond all ideas which will test ideas. That standard can function practically for us. It means that every institution, policy, plan, law and way of life has to be judged for its effects on the well-being of the Earth. Does it further, is it indifferent to, or does it harm that well-being? Finally, civilizations and values can be evaluated and verified as to whether they are truly cosmic, truly in accord with the grain of creation. As we reattune to our love of the Earth, our only home, we may be willing to make the necessary changes.

This is to propose that Earth is the new touchstone, a new

limit upon us, a standard from outside us. We have not had such a standard since Nietzsche declared "God is dead," meaning that there were no external standards on our behavior, no safety nets beneath us. Indeed, there is a standard upon us, very near and close to home, not a net under us but ground under our feet, and it can bring us to sanity in the ways that unlimited consumption, economic growth and the satisfactions of our desires never could. If we take the needs of the living, conscious, spiritual and divine Earth seriously, she will teach us the Dharma, the right order, of being human.

For what is the Earth? That part of the universe which is closest to us, our privileged vantage point upon the greater whole, our ready access to the divine in which we may step out, enter into, encounter and immerse ourselves. Cities are the artificial kingdom, in which all is fabrication and convention, but all around us lies the incarnation of God and the universe, waiting to bring us to health. And the Earth is very far from being an object, like objects we make, but is an infinitely deep and rich subject in her own right, with whom we have not even begun to take up relationship.

If we will turn to the Earth, the Earth which is one may quickly bring harmony out of our many conflicts. Think of the way two California grey whales trapped in Arctic ice recently united the Americans, Russians and Canadians. That is what the Earth is ready to do for us when we take her needs seriously. Human problems around the globe are now almost insoluble. The turn to the Earth will align our priorities, and give perspective on the issues which regularly inflame the passions in human society. Earth is one, and she will make a harmony out of our many.

To take an Earth-centered perspective on ourselves does not mean assigning priority to the biosphere over individuals, since no one yet knows how to measure the health of the biosphere. At the very least, the health of the biosphere is a function of the health of the individuals who make it up. And so, certain generalizations can be made. The most serious changes we are making to the Earth are to its chemistry. We are introducing chemicals which the Earth has not seen during all her five billions years of evolution, which are irreversibly changing the composition of the soil, air and water. You cannot have a healthy planet when you weaken the ecosystems with poisons, and humans must refrain from these practices.

We could build such a beautiful civilization on this blue-green planet of ours, as beautiful as that of early Greece, its white buildings surrounded by green forest and overlooking the wine-dark Mediterranean. Picture it: higher technology, clean technology, an agrarian society with vast tracts of wilderness retained or restored, where wild animals could live their serene and abundant lives; vital, alive cities, not like our present cities, doped and half-dead with their inhabitants crushed by routine; a world in which none have too much, and all have enough, the needs for food, clothing and shelter met, and the freedom to set about the spiritual and creative tasks of the truly human life.

We can have such a world, if we want it, with green forests, fresh air and blue, clean, teeming seas.

But if we are to have it, our societies are going to have to change their ways at every level.

From right ideas, right practices follow. We need leaders who can make their decisions as did the native peoples, "unto the seventh generation." We need to reorganize education, to root it in the Earth and the cosmos, in the new story of modern science, in an Earth-centered perspective, and we need to educate the right brain as well as the left, so that people may continue to experience the magic of childhood all their lives.

We need legal systems everywhere which recognize that Earth rights precede ours, that we are absolutely dependent on the Earth, and have no rights at all if she does not survive.

We need to put civilization on a whole new economic basis, which recognizes that the Earth is finite, has limits, that unlimited growth is simply not possible. Human economies have to be modelled on the great economy of the Earth, in which nothing is wasted, in which all benefit. There is no such thing as "throwaway" on a small planet. Our inflamed consumerism has to go through legislation which restricts the advertisers who are today primarily the ones responsible for inflaming our desires out of all proportion to our needs. Economists need to understand that in living systems such as the Earth is, processes are irreversible. Once we destroy all the energy-rich results of evolution, evolution will not recur, and we will inhabit a wasteland. On a living planet, we must ask of every "resource" before we cut, shoot, poison or net it, what function it serves for the whole.

Each of us has to "think globally, act locally" with respect to our own lives, asking of each item that comes into our homes, where it came from, who produced it, who made money from it, how many times it was sprayed, where it is going to end up. We need to return to basics. It is estimated that each middle-class North American home uses the energy of 350 servants. And people want more! Let us have a wise perspective on ourselves.

To take an Earth-centered perspective on ourselves means that we no longer go on forcing the Earth to support our diseased and inflamed civilization, but that we bring civilization into balance with the limits of the living Earth, and recover our own health, our own right order, by so doing.

Economically, practically, this means that as individuals and societies we must be absolutely clear on what we really need. What we really need is quite different from all our wants and desires, and means we give up the consumer wonder-world which is ravaging the planet. As Gandhi put it: There is enough for everyone's need, but not for everyone's greed.

As physical beings, we all need food, clothing and shelter. But just how much? Think how little space a tepee with a fire takes up, compared to our large, sprawling suburban homes down which is funnelling the energy of the planet. Clothing? A Carmelite nun once told me, with great joy: We have the simplest, most stripped down, bare life there is. I have only two habits; I never have to worry about what I am going to put on in the morning, and since I never look in the mirror, I never mind what other people think of me.

The Buddha observed: The more you have, the more you have to worry about. Possessions do not make for happiness; the folly of our age is to think we are only material beings. Possessions clutter the soul. Bare is beautiful, less is more; simplify your life-style and you find spiritual riches pouring in.

As physical beings, our needs are really very simple. But "No one lives on bread alone, but on every word that comes from the mouth of God." We are spiritual beings as well, and so we need time for the truly human creative and spiritual pursuits.

And that is all. But the world is at present mesmerized by glamour and hype so as to be unable to see just what our true situation on Earth really is. Our minds are full of ideas, words and things.

It is time to cut back to what we really need, that the forest may survive, that the plants and animals may survive. Such a move runs counter to the whole of economic practice, which is based on the assumption that the planet can provide us with unlimited goods, and is based on inflaming our appetites for things we do not need. But to be absolutely clear on needs is the very cornerstone of a sustainable economy.

Let us, all of us, create an economic revolution as a counter-force to the corporations. The present recession is a recession of the Earth from our assault upon her, and it will not disappear overnight. Let us meet the demands of an Earth which has limits by adopting a voluntary simplicity. Truly, we are at the time of great awakening. All of us have to wake up to the way we are being manipulated by advertisers and economists, by television and the media, and remember ourselves, take back our power, reclaim our sovereignty as members of the planet and take responsibility for living lightly upon her. Unlimited growth is inappropriate for the living being the Earth is, and it does not make for happiness. If all lived simply, all could live.

Finally, we need to revise our philosophies. Philosophy has always provided the guiding principles of civilization. Now it needs to provide those leading ideas which can bring civilization into balance with the living Earth, but modern philosophers, wholly out of touch with practice, seem not to know they live on a planet at all. Let them rally to the challenge.

The causes of the present crisis lie in our philosophical ideas. That crisis reveals that ideas really have a power philosophers have not always been aware of. Men and women take them up and live life on their basis. That is how ideas build civilizations. Let the philosophers be more careful.

And the crisis in the Earth adds a note about philosophical method. The Earth has not counted at all for philosophers up to now. The Earth gained value only as we "belabored" it or as it became "the substratum of our duty," a view which today fuels the activity of giant corporations. The Earth has always been verified by ethics, and ethics has been verified by a metaphysics of indubitable first principles, grounded in a transcendent and wholly unknowable "other," God.

The future will be rooted or it will not be (Charles Bell). This is the true order of priorities:

1. That ethics is verified which promotes the well-being of the Earth and all its inhabitants.
2. That metaphysics is verified which supports the ethics which supports the Earth. (The hope for metaphysics is that the Earth is part of the universe, the greater whole, and that in grounding ourselves on the Earth, we are only bringing ourselves to a finer, a more attuned relationship to the whole in that part of it which is accessible to us.)
3. That God is the right God who furthers the well-being of all creatures.

Those are some of the ways in which the Earth will readjust our thinking. Those are some of the transformations of consciousness which occur once we take the Earth seriously.

These are "the turnabout years" for the Earth. If humans do not change their present practices, the Earth may die, we along with it. We are approaching that point beyond which healing will be impossible.

There is only one imperative over all of us now: the planet must survive, and flourish, for she is the only home we have. We have to limit ourselves, to repair the damage we have done, and to assist the Earth in whatever way we can to heal herself.

You may ask why. I answer because the Earth is beautiful. As one who loves fierce winter storms, grey spring rains, purple twilight and dawn in a chorus of birds, I answer that this beautiful five-billion year old planet is our teacher. The human race has been in the "terrible-twos" ever since it arrived here, and

Earth is waiting to help us spin our cocoons and change from little worms into radiant butterflies. The Earth is beautiful, and we can be beautiful too.

The picture from outer space of the blue, green, gold and white Earth is our symbol, a mandala of wholeness. The human is at a distinctive phase of evolutionary development, and we have to solve the problems we are causing for ourselves and the Earth. Why? On behalf of magic.

Yes, there is an exquisite deep universe out there beyond the city lights, the concrete and glass, and it waits to bring human beings, worn down by a burnt-out world, to life, healing and wholeness. We have deep ways of communing and communicating with Earth, of taking up an I–Thou relationship with her, that we have never suspected before. The Earth is the body of the world's consciousness, and the devastation of the Earth reveals just how diseased our human consciousness really is.

It is the Earth we have left out of our philosophies all these centuries, the stone the builders have neglected, which is really the cornerstone. Now that her very survival is in doubt, we have to put her first, to take up a rightful, respectful place "as a part," that she and we may resurrect together.

Take heart. If the Earth is a living organism, she may possess great powers to heal herself. There are indications that even if we put a little energy into the Earth, the Earth bounces back. The people who cleaned up the Thames thought it would take twenty years for the salmon to return; they returned in five, and these results are being repeated elsewhere. We need to cooperate with her own desires for health.

The Spirituality of the Earth

Based on the ideas of the past—that animals are machines cleverly wired for sound, but have no interior life—we have almost done them all in. Let us, then, in the light of what we have said, provide new images for the Earth.

New Ideas about Plants

Plants are not "more primitive" than we are, but older and wiser than we are. They don't run about as we do. They are our teachers here. If we all lived on the moon for awhile we would know what plants give our world. Green. No wonder green is the color of healing and of hope.

Plants are crucial biologically. We and all the animals are totally dependent on fruits, flowers and vegetables, and the plants provide the oxygen we breathe. But the mystery of plants is deepening.

In *The Secret Life of Plants* (Tompkins and Bird) scientists describe experiments from which they conclude that plants feel, sense their environment, grow better with certain kinds of music, and pick up the unspoken thoughts of human beings around them. They visibly shrink if someone approaches them with the thought of doing them harm. They respond especially to children, perhaps because children are so clear.

The pioneer work on understanding plants is occurring at Findhorn, a community in northern Scotland devoted to understanding the spiritual dimensions of plants and the plant–human interaction. They have made some startling discoveries. The community was founded by three people who meditated, who heard voices in meditation advising them how to plant a garden. The first fruits of their efforts were twenty-pound cabbages grown on almost bare soil. The voices claimed to be those of Devas, angels responsible for plant life on Earth. They were extremely critical of the way we are using poisons, impairing plant vitality, and said if these practices continue, they may have to withdraw, finding their work impossible. Some of their methods for growing plants are described in *The Findhorn Garden*. The beauty of these methods is that they can be tried by all, in our own gardens. The proof is in the pudding.

Findhorn people notice that each plant has a different "personality," a different way of being, and that if one attunes oneself to the plants—stills one's inner being, one's thoughts and emotions, and attends receptively to the plant, it will fill the soul with a sense of its own being. Each plant has a very different consciousness, and reveals its essence to the inner senses, not the outer. Plants flourish when talked to, and sympathetically appreciated and loved. Such methods could revolutionize agriculture, which forces plants through chemical and other means. There may be more spiritual approaches to spiritual beings.

The Devas tell us more, that plants, simply attuned all day to the infinite consciousness out of which the universe comes, have Christ-consciousness. Most of us have not attained to such a state. Plants make that consciousness available to us. That is why being in a garden, or walking through the woods, is so refreshing.

What is key for us, is that plants, which most of us think of as lowly creatures, have brought us into contact with invisible spiritual realms, realms which have a great interest in life on Earth. Angels have been recognized since ancient times. This is the first modern contact with them. What is Earth, that they should care for her?

New Images for Animals

Who are the animals? We have turned them into little fluffy teddy bears and stuffed tigers for our children's cots, fur coats for women sensitive to fashion, food for our pets. We like them well, as long as they are transformed to meet our needs.

We have done all we could to distinguish ourselves from the animals, to separate ourselves from them. We are made in the image of God, they belong to Earth. But in truth, we are genetically related to them. Evolution makes us the first cousin of every living thing. We have similar cells, similar nervous systems, similar bloodstreams in which flow the early seas. We, like them, are wholly dependent on Earth.

Since Descartes we have thought of the animals as machines wired for sound. This tradition persists in the language of science. We reason and think; animals function by instinct and conditioned reflexes.

Evolution, our emergence from and through the cosmos, emphasizes our continuity with the animals rather than our separation. We are the keys to what they really are, just as modern scientists think they are the keys to what we really are.

In fact, animals are very much like us. They raise their young with love and affection, they are loyal to mates, when a mate dies, the survivor mourns, and like us, they learn all their important lessons through play. Anyone who lives with a cat knows it has personality, consciousness, self-consciousness. In fact, despite the theories of modern science, it dawns on almost everyone sooner or later that the animals are as conscious as we are, a consciousness very different from ours, but consciousness nevertheless. And in their ease within their own lives, the animals may just surpass us in the theological virtues of faith, hope and love. They have been here longer than we have, and they know how to live on Earth. They are our teachers here.

Animals know how to be alive. They know how to live in their bodies. For us, bodies are a means of transporting minds. But the animals can teach us Buddha-nature. Dogs know how to be out-of-doors, cats know when we are right with ourselves. The animals know how to sense the planet, to which we are essentially autistic. We cannot see, hear, smell anything in comparison with them. Animals know the beauty of the Earth. Only the human was expelled from paradise; the animals are still there. We stumble through the forest, seeing nothing but trees. Imagine how a deer or a rabbit sees the forest. Try experiencing the beauty of the pond as the frogs singing in the Spring experience it. We have to learn from the animals how to experience our beautiful blue-green planet aright.

We think of the animals as functioning by instinct. The animals must once have had to learn all that they know, both individually and as a species. It is improbable that they arrived on Earth knowing what their prey was and how to hunt it. What we call "laws of behavior" are really just the habits of mature beings. We try to teach the animals our language to find out whether they are "intelligent." We have no idea how animals communicate, and have not managed to learn the language of any animal yet.

And the spirits of animals! Like us, they have a psychic-spiritual dimension, they have their own complex inner lives. Having turned them into cuddly little toy bears, we have not the courage to confront the magnificent spirit of wild animals, the wolf, the deer, the fox, the Bengal tiger. The native North American peoples knew how to see that spirit, honored it, and were proud to be called "lone wolf" or "running deer." They still know how to see. That spirit is there, and we need to open our inner eyes. Every animal has its own distinctive form of consciousness, its own spirit. We have to recover ourselves as spiritual beings, and communicate with them.

The tragedy of the loss of species is theological as well as biological. The animals, too, are offspring of the creator, made in the image of the creator, embodiments of the consciousness of God. They all reveal something of the nature of God. When there are only cows and dogs and cats left on Earth, our children's children will know nothing of the glory of God.

The animals are a part of the complex, balanced ecosystem that Earth is, and form our life-support systems. Earth was not just aiming at the human, but at the whole, not one instrument but the complete orchestra. The animals are offspring of God and have rights as we do—rights to their habits, their migration routes, their nesting sites, their hunting grounds and their lives. We are now responsible for the planet. Our tasks are to live in harmony with all. To do this, we will have to learn from the animals.

For centuries, we have taken ourselves to be lords of the planet. In truth, we are the most dependent animal of all, utterly sustained by the plants and animals of the planet. Yet we treat them in the vilest way, not admitting our debt to them, not admitting they are our brothers and sisters. Meat-packing plants should be made of glass so we could all see the true cost of our insensitive way of life. Animals are in such terror during transport that they often die of cardiac arrest. How does an animal feel brought onto the killing floor? I imagine rather as the Jewish people felt entering Auschwitz. We have told ourselves animals have no inner life, no life of feeling. But they do.

It is time that we acknowledged the expertise the animals have in relating to the planet, and learn from them, our wisest and best teachers here.

The native peoples have a prophecy to the effect that there will not be peace on Earth "until the 2-leggeds marry the bear," that is, until we befriend all our 4-legged, winged and finned brothers and sisters, the animals.

Who Are the Trees?

Trees, likewise, are old and wise, our guardians here despite all we have done to them, and full of love for us. They bind soil, hold water, provide oxygen and water vapor for the Earth. In ways which the human does not yet understand, the old growth trees uphold the entire biosphere.

Trees were regarded as the enemy by early settlers, there merely to be cut down. The Findhorn Devas who attend the trees warn us that our insatiable greed for pulp and paper, for wood products, is endangering the life of the planet. The "harvesting" practices we follow—clear-cutting, replacing mixed-forest with tree farms of monocultures, not replanting, using herbicides and pesticides which poison the soil, ground water and streams—all this is total mismanagement. We have to change our ways. The forest does not mind giving wood; it does object to being murdered.

One can relate to trees as to plants; each tree has a different essence which it will reveal to an attuned consciousness. They also attune themselves to the infinite consciousness, and have Christ-consciousness. Stand before a tree and open yourself to it, and you can feel the love flow between you. Lean your back again an old maple, let your energies blend with its energies, and you will feel cleansed as though having received the eucharist. Trees, too, are spiritual beings.

So our new premises provide new images for plants, animals, trees—for dogs and cats, lupines, violets, pine and fir, for giraffes, penguins and the rest. The whole planet is animate and we need to see them through fresh eyes.

Nowadays, in our cerebral and intellectual world, the abilities to communicate with other life forms are considered a function of illness. These abilities are our birthright. We are aware that our children are seeing what we can no longer see. Our children are our teachers. We need to know that these deeper dimensions of experience are possible.

The whole planet is enspirited. "Ask of the birds, the beasts, the plants, the trees, that they might teach you the beauty of the Earth" (Paul Winter, *Missa Gaia*).

We have considered the living parts of the planet. Native North Americans regarded even the non-living parts of the planet, the rocks, the streams, the mountains, as enspirited, and so they are, all varying forms of God made manifest, all elaborated from the spiritual world out of consciousness, and they will touch our spirits if we let them.

So one can come to know the energy of the rocks, the water, the oceans. Let your imagination soar and your feelings open. We have regarded Earth as a mechanism for so long we have lost our capacity to be awakened by her.

What of the ecological zones? How different we feel in desert, in grassland, in rain forest. There are quite likely spiritual interactions, interactions through consciousness, between all parts of the planet. Each still lake, running river, each vast ocean, has its own spirit which refreshes ours.

We have not related to the planet as a spiritual being for a long time. To see it so is to begin to recover the magic of our Earth, far from facts and theories, directly touching our own spirit. Why, otherwise, are we so contented at the beach, so entranced by the high mountains which symbolize for us our vision? Thought has turned everything grey. The planet is waiting, through direct experience, spirit to spirit, to bring us alive again. Let us not destroy it when we are just on the verge of knowing ourselves through it. The planet experienced spiritually is waiting to enrich the life of the soul.

But we have to change all our ways; we have to become worthy of our divine Earth. At this point, only the Earth is holy, and not the human. The plants, the animals, all have their place, their order, their dharma; only the human is without. The taking up of relationship with the living Earth will show us our path. As we attune to the order that is in the Earth, very different from the order which predominates in our fabricated wonder-world, she can teach us the right order, the dharma, of the human.

A Touch of Metaphysics

Let us recapitulate briefly our history of ideas. There are many legacies of the Piscean age, not simply the last three hundred years which have birthed our modern world. There is something there in the world of art, literature, philosophy, for everyone. But metaphysically, the dominant legacy is dualism, and dualism has always de-divinized the Earth. Dualism ultimately comes from our creation stories which locate God outside the creation God makes. God is divine, creation isn't. The last gasp of this legacy has been atomism, mechanism and materialism. This is the appropriate metaphysics for the masculine form of consciousness which Jung characterized as aggressive, rational, logical, linear, judgmental, and non-relational. This is the form of intelligence which has dominated philosophy in the past, elaborated all our theories of knowing, being and doing, and elaborated present patriarchal civilization. The crisis in the Earth calls the entire tradition into question. The male impulse has come to the end of itself.

We have retold the creation story to make explicit the truth that God is in creation. Creation comes to be out of God and is an embodiment of God. Now we must say what it means that reality is spiritual. We shall draw up some major portraits of ideas, with bold strokes.

The Meaning of "Reality Is Spiritual"

Let us contrast materialism with the spiritual account given here. At the very least, to say that reality is spiritual means that consciousness precedes material form. Consciousness is energy and all energy has consciousness.

Materialism has been elaborated by male intelligence. What would civilization look like if elaborated by the feminine form? Jung described feminine intelligence as imagistic, poetic, imaginative, accepting, non-judgmental, non-linear, relational. This is a form of thinking which does not belong to women only, but is to be found in all of us. Feminism is a way of thinking and seeing. But it is no accident that this, a spiritual metaphysics, is being given by a woman, and it will help us, if we are to revision civilization, to keep these two very contrasting forms of intelligence in mind.

Dualisms always made of matter a lowly thing indeed. Aristotle called it *hyle*, a term of disgust, and distinguished the human from it. But if God is in creation, we are less distinguishable from creation. Earth is a form of God, and is fully animate, enspirited. Such is to give a very different interpretation of Earth, and to prepare the way for a "redirection of the gaze."

The tradition of the past, for the most part, is out of relationship. It contains only one book on relationship, Martin Buber's *I and Thou*. The patriarchal tradition, honed to its essence in the science-technology of recent centuries, has bequeathed to us a world in which our relationships, especially that to the Earth, are disordered. Right relationship is a task for feminine intelligence. Relationship, and all its subsidiary terms such as interconnected, interbalanced, ecosystem, is a feminine term.

What does it mean to say the planet is a spiritual being? It means there are two kinds of causality in the world. There is a way of being, and a kind of causality in the world, we do not understand, the causality of Spirit. Spirit is love, will, intelligence, all properties of the inner of things. Spirit is invisible, but most real, preceding things which shall all pass away. The real is perhaps unavailable to our usual senses. It is accessible to our spiritual senses, which modern people do not employ.

We know well the old mechanical causality, and there are good grounds for Descartes' distinctions. Pushes and pulls. It gets us to the moon, and to work on time. We know an ordinary causality of our lives, the linear horizontal order, the geometric, the routine of life.

But another causality, a kind of "vertical" order cuts across this. There are surprises of the Spirit, the reason C.S. Lewis called his autobiography *Surprised by Joy*. The touches of the Spirit are love and surprise. We are all familiar with a patterning of our inner states, our self-evolvement, the sudden gifts and awareness and coincidences which belong to another order. We are simply so taken up with the regular order we miss seeing this other. We miss what is really important. But it is this other which is prior, essential, the source of all meaning in our lives, the vertical order which gives us plot and purpose, the spiritual order in which the human dwells.

For scientific materialism, the world is inert. "Facts." On a spiritual level, the world is alive, and speaks to us with an ultimate speech. So St. Augustine, praying in a garden, heard children singing what sounded like "take and read." He took up the scriptures, and opened them randomly, and what he read there changed his life.

Materialism assumes that order emerges out of the parts. In a spiritual universe, there are quite likely long-range ordering influences in the planet, the cosmos, which bring harmony out of many different events and interactions, a whole which gently orders the parts. Who does not have the experience of being guided? Life goes along for the most part geometrically, and then some man, some woman crosses our path, and all is changed.

This means that our ordinary sense of things, all that the little positivist in all of us opts for, is not ultimate. It is a view of reality most comfortable to our human-centered perspective. But it is not final. The real is much greater than this, and we are ready to understand it.

The notion that this human-centered world is an appearance is an old one. It began with Plato. Plato thought the only way to know reality was through a flight of ideas up to first principles which he likened to the stairway out of our cave, a flight reserved to philosophers alone. We took this flight in our section critiquing the sciences as our ultimate story-tellers.

Like Plato, Kant also claimed that human beings lived in a world of appearances. He thought that the world had the form it had because of the constructions of our minds and sense organs. It was as though we were wearing purple-colored glasses and so we saw everything purple. From the true nature of things in space and time, we were excluded. We could never take off our purple glasses.

Human beings, for the most part, have never paid much attention to either of these philosophers. We take the world given to us by the senses as the real one. But now, modern physics is suggesting to us that these early philosophers were correct. Space, time and matter all merge together, and are in some sense, not "real." Stephen Hawking refers to "time (whatever that is)" (*A Brief History of Time*). Modern physics is preparing the way for the view we are advancing here.

Reality is a form of Spirit, and Spirit is much deeper than the "physical." It is out of sight. We can liken its being to an observation made by Descartes. All he sees going by his window are hats and coats. Are there human beings under them?

Our view has implications for knowing, which may be distinctly feminine ways.

For Kant, following Descartes, we could never know reality "as it is in itself." We were simply the mental spectators of matter, of "outsides." But we are more than this. I have named us "fragments of God."

Indeed, we are projections of God. We are all projections of infinite consciousness in the "physical." We dwell in depths of soul and spirit far beyond our minds. Everything else is a fragment of God, too, and harbors this deeper dimension. Our senses give us the outer world of trees, dogs, squirrels. The whole of science is based on sense perception, thinking and insight, but we have faculties for knowing which go beyond the five senses. These are our spiritual senses, our inner senses, little understood, designated by the distinctive term "intuition." Centuries devoted to reason know nothing about intuition, woman's distinctive term.

Emotions are channels of knowledge, but more than this, we have an inner being which taps into the world's inner being by its own faculties and methods. It is the soul. When we love another, revere another, honor another, when we are touched to our depths by music, by the ocean, we open to the world in a much deeper way than we usually do. The outer senses are the same. We have shifted inner levels. We are psychic-spiritual beings, as is the whole world, and the impenetrable stuff comes second.

That is to say that the outer world is a camouflage, an appearance, but that we are not inescapably confined to appearances, as Kant and Plato thought. If we are only minds in bodies, we would be. But all of us can have deeper forms of consciousness. We have an inner, and so does everything else, and the physical, which separates us, is really just a channel for connecting inners. Pascal said that the heart has its reasons, which reason does not know.

Plato's distinction between appearance and reality probably predates him, and haunts the history of philosophy, appearing in every age under new disguises. The truth is that Plato's "reality," often envisaged as another realm, could be construed in some aspects as the inner of things. This is a new understanding for philosophy.

For materialism, matter is opaque, and the most inner of scientific accounts—the atom, the electron—is, in fact, just another outside. Scientific explanations are like peeling the layers off an onion, the last one goes and you are empty-handed. There is nothing there. For materialism, there is only a material within. If consciousness comes first, there is a within of consciousness. It cannot be known through the senses as scientists employ them. It may be known directly, by heart consciousness, by intuition, by love and identification. One inner being reveals itself to another by ways which bypass sight and sound. Knowing is like a mother communing with her baby. Knowing is not "having a theory about," but communing and identifying with. New models for knowing are just one of the implications of our proposal that consciousness comes first.

Intellectual consciousness, the consciousness taught in schools, is primarily "head consciousness." True reality may only be accessible to heart-consciousness. Spiritual traditions attempt to develop heart consciousness, and for them, "reality" is something quite different than it is for the mind, for the distinctly male "separated" form. It is the consciousness of the North American Indians who marvelled that the white man always thought with his head, not with his heart. It is the form of consciousness most distinctive of the feminine, and is the form we all have to develop if the planet is to survive. We have to get in touch with how much we love the Earth, if we are to make our necessary changes.

In summary, the whole beautiful, seductive physical world is a camouflage of a reality much deeper, richer and more real.

Let us boldly, here, account for all origins. How does this all come about? We are entities in the spiritual world. We form a picture of the self we want to be, and the cells who want to be a part of that picture come along. These cells have their own forms of consciousness. They form an image of the reality they will share, and the molecules and atoms who want to be a part of that picture come along. The imagery is passed on down, and entities make their own free choices. What binds the many and the one is shared vision. It is likely that at the very bottom of the associations are entities which are pure consciousness, perhaps rendering the ultimate foundation of things, as Aristotle hoped it would be, transparent to intellect.

So, even our bodies are spiritual. So we have revised the premises of Descartes, and said, for the first time in many centuries, just what reality is. All matter is mind. The entire universe is formed from the consciousness of God. Matter is that consciousness in a highly condensed state, the consciousness of the human, animals and plants is the divine consciousness in a less condensed state, and God is pure divine consciousness. We live in a graded continuum of divine consciousness.

Heart consciousness, to identify it with the Earth, is our shamanic intelligence. We have not yet begun to know who we are, or what is available to us. The biggest mistake of the eleven seconds we have been on Earth may have been to take ourselves as minds and bodies, directed only outwards. The psyche has its own deep mystery, wisdom and knowledge. We tune out its knowledge because we believe we cannot have it. How great is the power of our ideas to keep reality out.

As Heraclitus, a pre-Socratic philosopher put it: You could not find out the boundaries of soul by travelling in every direction, so deep a measure does it have. Earth is waking us up to the truth about ourselves. We are all, everything here, projections of God. There are no atoms in the void, but we are, very deeply, all connected, with our source and with each other. All consciousnesses are interconnected.

What is consciousness? It is beyond the power of words to define. Consciousness is as a very brilliant color. This color both sends out its vibrations, its brilliance, and creates this brilliance through the absorption and radiation of light. It is as a light I offer this new, very simple classification of Being, to the ages.

All Is One

Our insights here stand in a venerable tradition. Heraclitus wrote about 2500 years ago: Listening not to me, but to the Logos, it is wise to agree all things are one.

He also left some other fragments which are corollaries of the view developed here:

> The things of which there is touching and seeing and hearing, these do I prefer.
>
> Eyes and ears are poor witnesses for those who do not understand their language.
>
> You would not find out the boundaries of the soul by travelling in any direction, so deep a measure does it have.

We have uncovered new premises for metaphysics, philosophy, Earth-thinking, civilization and for theology—let the next three hundred years not be nearly as impoverished spiritually as the past three hundred have been.

Now we return to science. Let us speak briefly of the modern passion for reduction in explanations, which is part of the baggage of modern materialism.

The goal of biology is to explain the structure and function of the animal in terms of the behavior of cells, and the behavior of the whole cell in terms of the structures and functions of the parts, the biochemical properties of its individual components.

It has been suggested that "living" may require a principle above and beyond the parts. The parts of different animals are all the same. What, then, makes for their differences? It is some principle of form. We have proposed that at the level of the human, consciousness precedes matter. That is to say, an organizing principle is present which does not emerge out of the parts, but which itself organizes the parts.

In the case of the human, we know the essential self is separable from the body, and that the body "dies" when that essential self departs. In the case of the human, there is an invisible, separable aspect of the human being which maintains the whole and departs from it at death. Life in the human has to be explained in terms of this spiritual reality, not in terms of the physical. The physical receives its organization from a nonphysical, but very real being. This is likely the case for all living beings, with whom the human is evolutionarily continuous.

The conviction of modern science is that the spiritual can be reduced to the living, the living to the physical. I propose that the order is just the inverse. This is to make a reduction "upwards." The domain of life may have to be explained by principles which belong to the spiritual. Intelligence, love and will do not come out of matter, they precede it, and they order it, as Plato suggested, "for the best."

Modern physicists are beginning to suspect design, teleology, in the universe. They cannot say yet just how this is present. The universe of earlier physics was "blind." It had no purpose. Now it is beginning to look as though there is purpose after all. Indeed, the proper analysis of classical experiments which "conserve energy" might show that the interactions cannot be understood without assuming some kind of what

Aristotle called final causality. It has been there all along, simply not recognized by physicists.

If Earth is a spiritual being, she is guided by intelligence, however we may finally spell out that intelligence. We may begin to suspect that Earth is unfolding a pattern of her own, in which we are meant to play a part. And so the question of the human place on Earth, and our true tasks here, become pressing, new questions about the human scene. We are projections of God who have forgotten our true nature, and fabricated a civilization around us designed to keep us in comfort and ignorance. But God is so close!

To put this another way: Spirit is the independent form of being, and "matter" is the dependent form. That is to say, everything we look at is built rather along the lines of this diagram.

In the very depths are the uncreated energies of God. These energies modify their way of being as they pass outwards and, at the outer surfaces, form the "outsides" we are so used to seeing. This cannot be quite the right description of beings, since all these energies interpenetrate. But there really are only beings, not things, not undifferentiated "matter" in the universe.

The universe is one in being entirely elaborated by Spirit, and in being forms of Spirit. Small dualisms remain—"mind" will always look different from "matter." But these are dualisms of standpoint, of which there are many. They are not, as Descartes claimed, dualisms of substance, interacting in the pineal gland.

That the universe is through and through conscious, spiritual, means that we are more at home here than we ever dreamed possible. The universe is more like us than we ever suspected. All faculties and abilities now regarded as unusual, explored by the fringes of culture, are our birthright.

The result of all this is that the universe is a much more wonderful, deep, surprising and imaginative place than just the visible. By far the most interesting things happen in the non-physical dimensions where the true causes for events originate. And the true principles according to which the universe functions are principles of consciousness. A whole new domain of exploration awaits us.

This is to realize, in modern times, what was realized by Heraclitus many years ago: Listening not to me, but to the Logos, it is wise to agree all things are one. Yes. Consciousness within consciousness within consciousness. That unity is not mechanical, not even organic, but spiritual in ways yet to be understood.

Modern civilization is built on materialism. We need a whole new way of viewing ourselves and Being, if we are to live in Earth aright. The cosmos is an elaboration of Spirit, Spirit's self-expression.

And so we turn to Stephen Hawking's question: *Why?*

The Answer to Stephen Hawking's Question

Stephen Hawking thinks he knows how the universe came into being. Now he wants to know: Why? Why did Spirit elaborate itself in such a vast array of beings? Yes, as Plotinus asked: Why did the One overflow?

This was a way for Spirit to know itself, to realize who and what it was in every way. Spirit is a living, creative being. We dwell in a universe which was made in love, which is good, which is suitable to every being who inhabits it. To be "made in the image of God" is to imitate God the creator and to know ourselves in our fruits.

Why has Spirit created the universe? Perhaps to give all of us a deep dimension of its dream, a kind of liberty we could never achieve if we remained part of the dream. And so, new ways to express itself, new possibilities for being.

What is the purpose of the universe? Simply to celebrate. To experience itself in as many ways as possible, to know itself, to celebrate itself. The universe is a place for delight. God made it for the fun of it.

Who are we? We are the celebratory animal. All the power of the big bang is in us, the God of the galaxies is within us, we are celebratory beings, we do it in our worship, we do it in our creating and we do it in our play. We do it in self-expression.

Indeed, the whole cosmos is a celebratory event. Our worship is just a participation in what is already going on, a recognition that it is already going on, and that that is what we are here for.

Yes, we are meant to play in all we do. As we celebrate, we celebrate ourselves, Earth celebrates herself in us, Spirit celebrates itself. As the spiritual sign of the Piscean age has been peace, so that of the age to come may be joy. In knowing the true nature of the universe, we have much to be happy about.

As fragments of Spirit, all the energies and the beauty of God are in us. As earthlings, all the beauty and life of the planet are in us. As cosmic beings all the energies of the big bang are in us.

The human being is today encased in a protective shell. We have not known who we are, because we have not known our story, because we have not done quite enough metaphysical questioning.

Now we have given all aspects of that story. It tells us that we are giants, living like pygmies. We are made for life in abundance, greatness of soul, expression of life, our truest, deepest selves and communion with the entire spiritual universe. We have reason to celebrate.

Modern unhappiness is primarily the result of living out false accounts of the universe. It also derives from having absorbed the pervasive image of crucifixion which dominates the west. (Catholics wear the body on the cross.) We do not believe we are made for happiness, and we do not know how to be happy. Why? Because God crucifies those God most loves.

Modern stories of the universe imply new spiritualities. Most of us still carry the billiard-ball model of reality in our minds. The modern atom is conscious, alive, empty space, more like an organism than a machine, something God could well come to us through. Modern physics is thus paving the way for a new spiritual sensitivity to Earth.

Indeed, new spiritualities are in order. Human beings have only been on Earth for eleven seconds on the scale of a twenty-four hour day. We are greater than anything we now take as being normal. Psychology is always monitoring averages. Perhaps Plato or Shakespeare should be our norm? The human race has been inwardly forming for a long time. Women are now appearing "up from under" the patriarchal carapace. We are ready for birth. The keys to our true spirituality lie in our bodies and in our emotions, our feminine functions, and their task is to bring to life the little child within us, the child left behind with the pre-Socratics at the dawn of patriarchy, the child buried under patriarchal ways. The child we all left behind in our haste to grow up.

That child dwells, inviolate, in the heart of our being. Women have always known how to nurture children. It is our feminine functions that will bring that child to life. It is the child which has heart-consciousness.

Earth waits for that child, and our new spirituality waits for it. For that child, so close to us, so recently come from God, dwells in the heart of our being, feeling, sensing, seeing and knowing the cosmos in all directions. And when we heal that child and set it free, we will know what it really is to be alive, and Earth will live with us, and within us.

The child lives within us like this:

Come now, do not despair. The God of the galaxies is with us. We have answered three of our four questions—the nature of the universe, God and the Earth. Now we approach the final question, ourselves. Who are we, amidst infinities, and what is the fullness of our true spiritual path?

God is . . . we are . . . and the story is unfolding within us. Put on a fresh, new spiritual way of thinking!

SPIRITUALITY

Healing Ourselves

To provide the self-image of the human is the most essential task of the Metaphysician.

—Emil Fackenheim

If we knew who we were we would know how to live.

A New Humanity

We have healed the false conceptions about the Earth we carry in our minds. If we act on the new conceptions—that Earth, far from being "mere matter," is a living, spiritual, conscious and divine being—then our practices will be right, and will bring human civilization into harmony with the planet. Now we have to heal ourselves. The Earth is alive; are we?

The spiritualities of the past have been elaborated on the basis of false views about the planet. We require spiritualities appropriate to a divine Earth, spiritualities appropriate to an Earth age. I believe our present ways of being are totally inadequate to the reality of the planet. We require a spirituality of resurrection.

It is the first week of native lore camp for children. Joshua Mensch, 12, came and sat with me on the steps of my hermitage tonight, and we listened to the wind singing through the trees. Joshua told me: I lose myself at school and at home. I miss the Earth. I really hope I can find myself out here this summer.

Let all who think the human is only a fabrication, entirely self-made, let all who think we are merely minds in bodies, come and sojourn with the Earth awhile. In the cities, we are fabrications in a fabricated world, our minds filled with detail, voices, words. Come, let the winds of Heaven wrap you round on a dark, mysterious night, star-laden, and let whispering trees and flowing waters fill your soul, cleansing it from the dross of civilization. Center down in a field of rustling grass, let the Earth restore you to who you really are, your deepest self, a self as old as the

Earth, a self even older, going back beyond the beginnings of life, a self without beginnings, rooted in eternal things of which the Earth is our nearest incarnation.

Let the Earth give you the Christ-self, the self that Jesus, fully incarnate in the Earth, realized.

For beyond all distinctions, you have a nature, and it is a great one. Some thinkers are calling this the ecological self. Earth has the keys to realize it.

Why are we destroying our beautiful five-billion-year-old blue-green planet? Because we do not know who we are. No one has ever told us the truth about ourselves; indeed, only now can it be said. We have not known the true nature of the human condition, and we have taken out our frustrations on Earth.

We have spoken of a new universe, a new heaven and a new Earth. Who are we, to live among them? It is time, now, to speak of ourselves, the newcomer to the planet.

Who are we, then?

We Are the Animal Who Celebrates

We are the celebratory animal, formed of the dust of Earth and the breath of heaven. Teilhard de Chardin calls us the universe reflecting on itself. Why does the universe want to reflect on itself? Because it is so beautiful, so mysterious, so fathomlessly deep. We are the celebratory animal. We celebrate in worship. At the end of an arid, patriarchal era, a cerebral, analytic era, we want to dance, praise and adore. We want to set free all our faculties and energy.

We also celebrate in creating. We create. Worlds invisible. The patriarchal era which is just ending has realized, magnificently and for all to see, the creative aspect of the human spirit, the human spirit as creator, made in the image of God, giving form and expression to what had meaning for it. We have done this in paint, in stone, in the written word, in music and in drama.

So, in a scientific era, we give form to our experience of the universe in laws, in formulas, in theories. Our knowing is a "giving form" which we hope corresponds to the forms in things, and is thereby true. Now we situate that order-making in the context of the greater story. We are the creature who tells itself its story, that we may know who we are. We have formed an outer identity. True identity is taking shape in the inner, which is beneath it. We are ready, increasingly ready, for that true spontaneity which is founded on long moral and spiritual discipline. We are formed. It is time to set aside our training exercises, and be.

Why must we create? The Delphic oracle prescribed: "Know Thyself, and you shall know God and the universe." We can only know ourselves in seeing our fruits. God made the universe, a form of God's self-expression—fullness of identity. God is not finished; God has not begun to realize God-self. We are one of the places where that self is realized in ongoing creativity. We have ravaged the planet on false theories, on the misdirecting of energies. Now we have to outstrip all previous creativity, in becoming co-creators with God of a civilization in balance with the planet.

Could it be that we were meant for joy? The universe is a metaphor for the human, and the human for the universe. The universe celebrates itself. That is its reason for being. We are participants in that celebration, and there is an energy in us purely for praise.

For we are bigger, deeper than we know. And all our ways are holy.

We Are Earthlings

We are formed of the dust of the Earth, we are earthlings. The early seas flow in our bloodstreams. We are made up of masses of squirming cells, organized in interdependent relationships. Every cell is living, and must be perpetually nourished by taking in food. Our food comes from the Earth, is our connection to Earth even in the heart of our greatest cities. We are not "lords of the Earth," but utterly dependent on Earth, who nurtures us.

Ancestral memory is deep in us. We have sojourned long on this planet, we are one with her, and we have encoded in our bodies her ancient rhythms of night and day. We know the meaning of sunrise, and darkness, of new moon and full moon, of winter solstice and spring equinox. Everything on the planet, which we have known for centuries, is a symbol for us of our life here, appearing nightly in our dreams. We know the meaning of our own symbols because it is rooted in the deep knowledge our psyche possesses about the meaning of events on this planet. We have sojourned in her for millions of years; all our cells, our nervous systems, go back to the beginning of things.

What does it mean to be earthlings? To be deeply anchored here, not with our conscious minds, but with the whole unconscious knowledge of our bodies of what it is to be on Earth, whose conditions we know absolutely with a knowledge far beyond our power of access. That is why, when we walk out in a field, or stand within a glade of trees, our bodies remember who they are, who they really are, and we know through our bodies what we are doing in being, not with head knowledge but with a knowledge so deep it is beyond all speech. Earth is our first, our oldest home.

All our previous spiritualities have been "high in the head." Our virtues have been the virtues of men, connected with Logos; our values have been those of thinking and reasoning, out of relationship with life.

The human being has fabricated for itself a heavy casing, a shell which must split open if we are to grow. The appearance of women on the historical stage is the first crack in that shell; taking up relationship with the Earth is the second.

We are a part of Earth, even when in the depths of our fabricated civilization. We are wholly nurtured, nourished, sustained by her. We are in a relationship of total dependency upon her, and to be aware of that relationship to her, of all the distinctive ties, is the beginning of the way to spiritual health.

The real joys of life come to us through our bodies, those bodies which transport our minds from place to place, but in which we do not yet live. True knowing does not emerge high in the mind, but low in the body. Prayer has its bodily effects, and whatever mysterious composite we are finally declared to be, the body anchors us into the present. When we are most grounded, we can be most with God.

And we share so much with the animals. Our homes, what are they but shelters, like dens, holes and nests. Let us remember, when we compare ourselves with the neighbors, that homes are just shelters from the elements, places to bring back little stones and twigs which have meaning for us. Clothes are a substitute for fur, each outfit expressing the essence of the soul. Our courtship behavior most resembles that of the birds, where it appears to be constant appeasement, reassurance of non-aggressive intent.

Eating, making waste, raising young from painful birth with love and attention, passing on skills, enjoying the Earth, sharing mortality—we share everything with the animals, bound like them to blood and bone and dreams. All of us—earthlings.

We are aspects of Earth. In us, Earth lives out more of her fathomlessly deep ways of being conscious of herself. Always, for us, the imagery of the Earth flows in our souls. Oh, who will go for her? Who will celebrate the glories, the mysteries, the magic of the Earth as Dante celebrated heaven? Our belief systems divide us from one another; it is our life as earthlings that will make us one.

We Are Fragments of Spirit

We are formed of the breath of God, fragments of Spirit incarnating in the Earth. How deep do we go? We are very deep. All the principles and powers of the whole cosmos, the energy of the big bang, the wisdom which orders the parts aright, the depths of space, the beauties of the night, are in us.

Just how deep are we? How deep do our psyches go? Into the great web-work, the hidden spiritual realms and underpinnings of the cosmos. On our inner sides we extend inwardly into the great fathomless life of the universe, but we are all taken up with appearances.

One consequence of being so deep is that we have many faculties for knowing that we are not at present using—our inner, spiritual senses, about which we know almost nothing. People have assumed that because they cannot see spiritual reality, it is not there. There is a positivist in all of us, who would like to believe the physical is all there is. Spiritual reality disdains the encumbrance of sense. But we are spiritual beings, and this dimension of our universe will contact us through channels other than the senses.

Now we know that Spirit precedes matter, that the universe is essentially spiritual beings, that there are quite likely other levels of spiritual existence beyond the human, which we can communicate with. We can open up to our true dimensions.

If Spirit is first, if all reality is a form of Spirit, if there are other dimensions than the physical in the universe, if most of ourselves is, in fact, out-of-sight, hidden from us, it seems quite likely that there are other spiritual beings, communicating with us, besides ourselves. We have neglected the "higher" invisible realities just as we have neglected Earth. This may have been necessary in order to build a sense of human identity. Now the universe is drawing back its veils. We are on the edge of startling new discoveries about just how vast the cosmos and ourselves really are. We will begin to live when we live from our inner sides, from the ebb and flow of our energies, rather than notions of what we "should" be.

As fragments of Spirit, all the wisdom and knowledge of the entire universe is in us. With what assurance then we should proceed in life, drawing on our deep unconscious knowledge, the knowledge embodied in our cells, in our billion year old nervous systems, in the depths of our souls, in our genetic codes. In the depths of our souls flows the great life, the memory of God for which nothing is forgotten, nothing is ever lost.

The Delphic oracle said to know yourselves, and you will know the universe and God. Ah, but there is a knowledge that is not head knowledge. It is a way of being. To this, we have to come.

What are we meant to be? Fragments of God, fully incarnating in our bodies in the physical, with all our inner senses open, and deep knowledge of identity. Our task is to embody God here.

The spiritual sign of the Piscean age is peace, and a certain peace there is in all crucifixion. The true symbol for us, for an Earth age, is the perpetually dying and perpetually resurrecting Earth. Ever and again, Spring follows Winter. And as the sign for the previous age was peace, that of the coming age is joy. For all is now accomplished.

Heart Consciousness

All that has been said indicates that human beings are very large indeed. We are giants. But at present, we are not living any of this. We are not living the truth of our own natures. We are giants, living like pygmies.

What are we supposed to look like? Like Christ. St. Paul called Christ "the first-born of many brothers and sisters." In particular, after crucifixion of our spirits by materialism these past three hundred years, we are meant to look like Christ resurrected, to pulse with that confidence, purpose and sense of life.

It is no secret that we don't. For the most part, we take our shape from convention, custom and the constraining glance of others, not from the cosmos or our own inner blueprint.

Why have we lost our intimacy with the planet? Why can we no longer feel the ground under our feet, touch the bark of trees, sense the magic of winter storms, smell the sweet scents of the Earth after a rain, taste our food, delight in our bodies and live in them?

It is because we are so wounded. We are wounded by the false ways of the past, by the false ways of our own civilization. Our minds have been fettered by false conceptions of the Earth and our life in it, our hearts and souls are in bondage, our bodies are the prisoners of our uptight conventions about manners.

And this is all because our inner child is not alive. The inner child lives, sensing, seeing, feeling all things, inviolate at the heart of our beings. It is time we brought the inner child alive, in our personal lives and in the life of civilization.

The twentieth century has been about beginnings and depths. Besides the new story, the other great discovery of our century is the inner child; just how much of the wounds of childhood, when we are most vulnerable, live on in our adult psyche, keeping us captive to the past? The child in us lives on in the heart of our adult beings, bound and fettered, never allowed to express itself. This century has given us ways to heal and set free that child, to let it express itself, and to release its prodigious energies. The inner senses, which reveal to us the true depths of reality and open us to the loving energies and knowledge of the spiritual world, are in that child.

How do we reach this child? Through the heart, as contemplative prayer traditions have always known. Christ was a heart-conscious man who loved little children. Patriarchal consciousness, cerebral consciousness, is in the head, and does not sense the Earth which supports and sustains its thinking. This is the "separated" consciousness so prevalent in modern times. To it, the world would look better paved, converted to suburbia and parking lots, grey, not green.

Heart-consciousness is the unity consciousness of being, accepting, affirming, non-judgmental. It characteristically belongs to "unalienated" women, to native people, and to Christ. Prayer puts you in touch with it, and it is the gateway to the infinite dimension of our beings. Heart-consciousness is the connected form. Only a consciousness based on the heart can see the spiritual dimensions of our life. Put your head in your heart and you will know the will of God for you.

The mind thrives on distinctions, the heart unifies. Intuition, so often identified with women, is the voice or the wisdom of the Infinite in us. Intuition is a form of knowing which comes through the heart, the emotions, the love-emotions, heart-consciousness. It has never been analyzed. It does not proceed by inference, argument, logic or proof. It is a pure identification and communion with the object, a connection with the "inner" of events and beings, a connection unavailable to mind and the senses. This is God's way of knowing, and it is one of our faculties. The heart is the gateway to the spiritual dimension of the universe. One of the oldest ways of getting in touch with it is simply the Jesus prayer, simply "Jesus, Lord Jesus," coordinated with the breathing, and placed mentally in the heart.

All spiritual paths must divest consciousness of the concepts of wonder-world, and today that is a patriarchal wonder-world. As Plato put it: There comes a time to take off the blinkers. If one wants to know the ways of the infinite, there is a path. One must align one's consciousness with it, source of our beings, rather than the world. One must get in touch with one's deep inner side, one's eternal self. The spiritual is not a fact to be taken over; you have to learn to see it.

Heart-consciousness, women's consciousness, native consciousness—knowledge of the sacred in all its ways. When you get in touch with the heart, you get in touch with the whole feeling and emotional life which has been suppressed by reason in a patriarchal world. And with the life of feeling, the inner child begins to stir. That child is the Christ of our beings, beyond space and time, knowing truths hidden since the foundation of the world, being born in a stable.

Inner Child

Inner child has the necessary sensitivity to Earth, and inner child alone knows the way to the heart of the Father, who is really the beloved.

The spiritual traditions know much about the divine within us, and modern psychology knows much about the human within us. It is time to bring these two traditions together, to heal our psyches. Jung thought that one's ease or dis-ease in nature reflected the health of one's relationship with one's own unconscious. These insights are beginning to be made available to all through the writings of his disciples, and to be disseminated on a larger scale.

The unconscious, and with it the emotions and the feeling child, has been suppressed by a patriarchal civilization which always valued "Reason." Now, with the inflow of the feminine principle, when humanity is about to take a giant evolutionary step, from Winter into Springtime, God is healing our emotional lives. It is as though the human race had to separate itself from nature and from its unconscious life, in order to establish identity. Now, with identity secure, it must return to heal the wounds it has incurred along the way, and retrieve the neglected parts of its psyche. This is so for the world as a whole, which is having to admit the feminine, the emotional and feeling life, to its thinking, and so for each of us.

As one begins to develop heart-consciousness, the first dimension of one's psyche to appear is the inner child. Let me say something about my own experience of inner healing.

I grew up in the household of a physicist, asking all the questions of children which, typically, physicists can answer. "What makes the rainbow?" "What makes the clouds stay up?" Later, I studied science through the Ph.D. level with the conviction it could explain the universe. Deep into my studies, I discovered that it could not explain the universe—all scientific explanations rest on "unexplained explainers."

I then turned to the study of philosophy for answers. While teaching the great books of the western tradition at St. John's College in Sante Fe, New Mexico, I visited a nearby monastery. I took one look at the faces of the men and women there, and knew they had the truth. But what did they have? I returned many times to find out, and joined them for a time to deepen into it.

Now I must tell you that my search was not continuous. Between finishing my studies of science, and taking up the study of philosophy, there was a night of pure terror—all the emotions of childhood welling up—in which I walked into a nearby mental hospital and signed myself in. The terror was gone in two days, but they kept me there for five months in order, as they put it, to "stabilize" me. I was kept on a locked ward with severely depressed older women. I was twenty-seven at the time.

As a result of that hospitalization, I developed almost unbearable "free-floating anxieties" which were to persist in me for the next ten years, until I experienced deep inner healing in the monastery I mentioned, the Benedictine and Charismatic monastery of Pecos, New Mexico. I studied and I taught during those years, but I was afraid of everything, of everyone and of going anywhere alone. It was like living in a fire.

At Pecos, I learned something about the nature of the spiritual world, about the Lord as a healer of souls, present today as ever (everyone in the room at mass could feel the wonderful warm presence which swept through it, and which people called the Lord). I witnessed for myself the many physical and mental healings accomplished by prayers with the laying on of hands, and came to a knowledge of Jungian analysis of the soul and the interpretation of dreams.

But I experienced, especially, deep prayers for the inner healing of the child we all carry within us, for the early wounds of childhood, which set me free from the anxieties I had carried with me for the previous ten years, and put me on a path to healing, wholeness and attunement to Earth which I have followed ever since. I want to share with you some of my understanding of inner healing and the ways the Holy Spirit works with us which comes from that time.

We all come to the Earth plane from spiritual dimensions of the universe, as a fresh, loving child, containing within it all the power and energy of God. We come from unlimited dimensions, into the limited boundaries of a small body, the experience of learning about the physical and incarnating within it, and the warped belief structures of our civilization.

We encounter the expectations of parents, siblings, teachers and schools. We mold ourselves, hiding our true beings under masks to suit these expectations of others, and later, as adults, we live in society almost entirely conditioned by what others will think. We are all deeply scarred. We are all covered over with layers of adaptation.

Our real self is still there, living in the heart of a little child at the center of our beings, a child who is perfectly OK and knows it, and who, now that we are grown up and have "identity," knows who we are in the world, simply wants to express itself about all that has happened to it, releasing itself from those emotional bonds. The ascending path into fullness of being can only be accomplished by the descending path into the center of our own souls, where living waters flow. Most of us no longer believe we have souls, we are so fettered up. Christ was an unfettered man, living from the heart.

At Pecos, such healing was done in the presence of the Lord, who is a very real power one can feel flowing through one when praying for another. We prayed through old emotional bonds and blocks using imagery of the risen Christ. Essentially, very insignificant events in a loving community would open the old wounds and painful memories—senses of rejection, separations, early hurts and anger. Everyone there understood themselves to be on a path known only to the Spirit of bringing to life the Christ within, who lives in the heart of that little child. The process was one of taking off bandages. Each of us was like Lazarus, called forth from the tomb, and now others undid the wraps.

The experience of inner healing is the most beautiful there is. We can feel the knots in ourselves. As knots in myself were undone and I prayed through the old pain with members of the community in imaginative images, I could feel living waters flowing within where before there had been only aridity. Our inner depths are real, and civilization will have to reckon with them if it wants to take the next step. Each one of us is ready to take it. Children are nature-mystics, and that is what we are coming to be.

Christ spent most of his time out of doors, prayed in the mountains, found in Earth rich imagery and parables for the spiritual life. Christ was a man at ease with himself, and with Earth. So we will be.

Afterword
Portrait of the Metaphysician

All must make a unity of
themselves. Some only have
very difficult starting
materials.

—*Ludwig Edelstein*

Now, the Metaphysician must put down her pen.

She thanks all, for all have contributed—on the subways, on the city streets, in the newspapers, in restaurants. Now she will disclose to you the Way of the Metaphysician.

My Way has been prayer. Prayer opens one to the inner depths, and makes available to one the power of the universe. I have tried to be a channel for that power.

I have come to this view of the universe by the mediation of powerful identities. I discovered, through long brooding and rumination, and sudden insights while doing the ironing, walking in a park or getting on a bus, that the most essential and basic concepts of whole separate fields of discourse refer to the same things, Being is Life is Spirit, the Inner Child is the Inner Senses, and so forth. These identities have formed for me the ascending stair to the New Vision of the Universe which I have presented here.

The ramifications of this New Vision are already taking

shape. For the time being, the Metaphysician must put down her pen in order to arrive at that wholeness the Metaphysician is ever seeking—balance between the inner and outer, thought and speech, word and being, higher and lower—all reconciled in a word, *the* word which guides her way: *fullness of being,* of all kinds.

So I summarize our argument. Inquiry, in all branches of learning, occurs in the same way, human beings grow in the same way, civilizations change in the same way. That way was given essentially by Socrates in *The Phaedo.* Choose the idea which seems to you the best, gather to it those which agree with it, and live life on their basis.

Yes, let life go forward on it. An idea is a way of giving life form. Your understanding of life will be satisfactory for a while, and then new experiences will come into it, novel experiences, new data as it were, and the old conceptions will prove inadequate. For a while you will be in a blur, and then, mysteriously, new and more adequate conceptions will come your way, for all is "given" in this universe which is gradually lifting its veils for each one of us.

This is the way of what is called "dialectic," which produces and forms our vision of reality on the fruitful tension between ideas and the lived life, forming ourselves in the process. The bringing of ideas into the lived life, and the testing of them there, produce for all of us what Plato and Hegel called the ascending path of dialectic. For Plato, it was the path reserved to the very few among the philosophers, a path of ascending to the truth by critiquing fundamental first premises. We have all been doing it in these pages.

So civilization has been proceeding on the distinction of Descartes between Mind and Matter, and his contention that Matter is devoid of Mind. The crisis in the Earth has forced us to go back and dig up this hidden premise of our lives, and I have rewritten, here, Descartes' notion of Matter. Essentially, it is: No Matter Without Mind. All Matter is enspirited. The whole cosmos is, once again, animate. Earth is not "matter"; there are no "things," there are only beings with consciousness. All beings have an essential inner dimension, consciousness comes first and forms the outer.

We have said more. Matter *is* Mind. The physical is simply consciousness in a highly condensed form, the consciousness of Spirit incarnating in the Earth. Those are the new premises, the new assumptions which I have proposed that will lead us to a true understanding of the universe, and a new sense of ourselves.

And antedating Descartes' distinction, we challenge the more fundamental distinction of Aristotle between matter and form, which underlies the *Summa Theologica* of St. Thomas Aquinas.

Dialectic is the way we live our lives. We are bundles of beliefs which we hang on to, which form a secure structure for our identities, many of which are collective and about which we order civilization. But we are basically explorers and adventurers, and we are always pressing beyond the "authorities," even our most cherished own. We gradually outgrow old ideas as we come to better ones.

What are better ideas? Those more adequate to our new maturity. Those which help all human beings, and all life everywhere, in all forms, to flourish.

So, in this work, we have taken the turn to the Earth after centuries of gazing heavenwards. We turn to live *here*.

It is no accident this turn is being made by a woman. Women have long been identified with Earth, and shared her fate. But I pay tribute to my brothers. We had to find our way through the new cosmology of our day, a twenty billion year story in time, to know what the Earth is.

Tom Berry calls us "fossilized stardust." We are part of the universe, the cosmos. We are cosmic beings, dwelling on Earth.

We are part of the Earth; the Earth is part of us, our closest vantage point on the greater whole.

The Earth is, together with ourselves, an embodiment of divine energies.

These are simple things to say; their implications, for the way we think about God and ourselves, for the way we *relate* to

God and the Earth, are immense, for what we thought available only in Heaven must be available here. God is waiting, under a thousand accidents of form and color, to touch each one of us directly. We are meant to be happy on Earth! Every being on Earth is a form of consciousness, and within every distinctive form of consciousness is the consciousness of God. God is here, God is so close, God is with us. It is time to leave behind the centuries of fear and separation, for love and connection, the ways of the spiritual world we are meant to realize here.

So, in this work, we have left behind the distinctions, the splits and separations of the previous age, for the *unity* consciousness of Being, and some of its many implications for living. We have presented, in short, a *Feminine* consciousness of Being. We have come to it through the ascending path of dialectic.

So it is with the great knowledge of identity, of the Feminine, emerging among women. One woman writes a work out of her experience, revealing her Muses, and with her achievement out there in finished form comes a challenge and a dare: come higher.

Basically, we are climbing companions, all of us, climbing higher and higher in the mountainous territory of Being, Truth and Eternity. Each work done, wrought in pain and usually followed by depression (which is really a dark night of the Spirit) is a piton nailed into solid rock, below which we cannot slip back, which yields for us a firm footing and provides a whole new sense for what our lives can *be*.

My life owes much to Athena for the bright sword of intellect, to Artemis for the Earth, and to Persephone for the long voyage underground.

It owes even more to the Lord, who is my chief guide.

But I want to pay tribute here to a very special woman, Virginia Woolf, who contributed so much to knowledge of the Feminine.

It was Virginia who said: Women's works descend from their mothers.

For Virginia, it was Jane Austen; for me, it was Heraclitus (Heraclitus taught me to see, and alerted me to the soul's depth).

All of us wonder about Virginia, in the midst of the battle

at its outermost point, warrior woman. Virginia dared to put her beautiful woman's nature forward, to be mocked and scourged by the critics and the most vicious temperaments of her day, on behalf of all of us.

I want to pay tribute here to Virginia Woolf, author of *A Room of One's Own*, who changed my life, that very great spirit who lived among us for sixty years. She never fully managed to net that black fin appearing in the sea of her imagination to her inward eye, that fin which always signalled the onset of another psychological breakdown. I believe she had experienced trauma in her early childhood which only now do we know how to heal.

We all wonder about Virginia.

I venture to say of her: She is, like the ancient prophets and martyrs, one of those of whom God asked everything, because God knew she would give everything.

Ave atque vale.

Now, the Metaphysician takes her leave of you. These heights, these splendid vistas that the mountains provide, are too much for her. Rilke: Terror is the beginning of beauty we are not yet able to bear.

She returns to the inner waters where she, being the Fish, is most at home. Her life of prayer and simple dwelling in the Earth.

When she addresses you again, it will all be in much simpler terms. She asks you to learn, by that time, that the trees channel to us the thoughts of God.

Until then, Peace.

There is nothing I know to compare with the delight of the living waters of prayer, in which God reveals to the inner being, without concepts or images, who and what God is. I return to the inner life which I love, in all of Being, the very best of all.